G. Hardt-Shirikwa

JESUS
IN CONTEMPORARY
HISTORICAL RESEARCH

IN CONTEMPORARY
HISTORICAL RESEARCH

by
Gustaf Aulén

Translated by
Ingalill H. Hjelm

FORTRESS PRESS Philadelphia

Translated from the Swedish *Jesus i nutida historisk forskning*, 2d ed., (Stockholm: Verbum, 1974). Copyright © 1973 by Gustaf Aulén.

Biblical quotations from the Revised Standard Version of the Bible, copyrighted 1946, 1952, © 1971, 1973 by the Division of Christian Education of the National Council of the Churches of Christ in the U.S.A. are used by permission.

COPYRIGHT © 1976 IN THE ENGLISH TRANSLATION BY FORTRESS PRESS

Library of Congress Catalog Card Number 75–36451
ISBN 0–8006–0438–5

5357E76   Printed in U.S.A.   1-438

CONTENTS

FOREWORD

A great many books have been written on Jesus. This is no less true today than at any other time. This book is, however, as far as I know, a new approach to the subject. I have concentrated my examination on the historical-critical Jesus research of the last decades. Since I am not myself an exegete, my intention is not to make pronouncements on the basis of my own study of the sources as to the historical trustworthiness of the gospels' descriptions of Jesus. The task I have set for myself is rather to examine the results which a few representative scholars have arrived at in their attempts at mastering the sources. This approach to the subject does not necessitate entering into intricate debate concerning the methodology of Jesus research. If methodological questions are touched upon here and there, it is not the working method but rather the result of that method which is important. All the authors on whose work I have relied are well recognized.

The literature in this field is extraordinarily rich and I am fully aware that I have not been able to treat all relevant writings. Yet I believe that those authors whose voices we shall listen to give a representative picture of the present situation in research.

The books which are the object of study here have all been published since 1960. This demarcation in time has been made not only because I have the present situation in mind, but also because the last decades have seen a change in the research situation which still dominated in the middle of this century. Extreme points of view have been toned down and certain converging trends can be observed. This matter ought not to be exaggerated. It is no more possible now than it was earlier—with regard to historical trustworthiness—to write a biography of Jesus or psychologically to analyze him. There are a great many opposing interpretations, not only concerning details but also concerning fundamental questions. The wide uncertainty which still exists in this field must certainly be acknowledged. If one approaches exegetical research from the perspective of other areas of research (in my case many decades of work in the history of Christian thought and systematic theology) the question in need of an immediate answer is whether and to what extent it is possible to differentiate between that which is uncertain or inaccessible and that which can reasonably claim historical trustworthiness.

The intention in this book is to show—in spite of all the uncertainty—that within a certain framework scholarship has arrived at a consensus which testifies to a degree of historical trustworthiness. This concerns above all two important points: Jesus' radical proclamation, and his message of the breaking forth of the kingdom of God which he proclaimed in his deeds. In the last chapter of the book I shall summarize and comment on the result.

The problems surrounding biblical research are enormous and plentiful. None of them is more important and at the same time more difficult to solve than that which concerns Jesus. During this century we have experienced a period of radical skepticism when scholars did not dare write books on Jesus, and this refusal both opened the way for a variety of inferior writings about Jesus and also tried to make us believe that it was quite irrelevant—at any rate for Christian faith—whether we knew or did not know anything historically trustworthy about Jesus, his proclamation, and his mighty acts. Such reasoning is totally unrealistic, a chimera, a kind of hide–and–go–seek. Even though it is uncontestable that Christian faith as such rests on another foundation than that of Jesus research, Christian proclamation and instruction cannot live in isolation from this research. Experience proves, in reality, that we are dealing here with a dialogue which can certainly be filled with tension but which at the same time is fruitful. The problems of Jesus research must also be seen from a purely human interest: Jesus is a central figure in the history of mankind and it therefore remains a most important question whether historical-critical scholarship can give us trustworthy knowledge about him.

Lund, Sweden   GUSTAF AULÉN
Fall 1975

1

ORIENTATION

Purpose

The intent of this book is to present certain conclusions which contemporary historical-critical research has reached concerning the earthly
Jesus.[1] For reasons which will be accounted for later, I shall limit
my analysis to important works which have appeared since 1960. Our
question is: on the basis of current research, what can we know about
the earthly Jesus? What is historically trustworthy?

In concentrating on strictly historical-critical research I shall refrain
from dealing with the rich and multifaceted flood of literature about
Jesus which has appeared alongside the work of scholars, and which
we meet in all sorts of attempts—with both positive and negative intentions—to draw a picture of the man who is simultaneously hidden and
illuminated by the stylized description in the gospels. When I leave
this literature aside, it is not because it is uninteresting. On the contrary, it arouses a great deal of interest, chiefly because it invites a
spontaneous and personal reaction to the gospels and especially to the
human figure of Jesus. Contemporary writings of this kind provide
much thoughtful information about our current religious problems.
But if one wishes trustworthy information concerning what is historically valid, one must turn to historical-critical research, which
proceeds on the basis of strict methodological principles. It would
be without rhyme or reason to turn a deaf ear to whatever might be
learned from the enormous and conscientious research which has been
carried on during this century—not the least of which has been done
during the last decades—if one intends to seriously come to terms with
that problem which is at once the most important and the most insoluble of all issues in biblical research.

Can one really know anything about the earthly Jesus? Since that
which can be tracked down concerning him from sources outside the
New Testament is minimal and unimportant, one is limited to the New

1

Testament writings. But here we immediately meet with difficulty, in that all of these writings are confessions which bear witness to the primitive church's faith in Christ. They are all deeply impregnated with the primitive Christian faith in the resurrected and living "Christ." That which is reported about Jesus in the gospels appears in this context and is marked by the titles of honor which were later given to the Lord of the church. There are clearly extraordinary difficulties in penetrating back to the primitive and authentic figure of Jesus. Such research may well be compared to an attempt to restore a painting which during the course of time has been covered over with other colors. This comparison has limited value, but in any case it gives an idea of the kind of work involved.

At any rate, scholarship faces what appears to be a hard, if not insoluble, problem. During the decades since about the 1920s, dominant research has reached conclusions extremely skeptical of the historical validity of any positive statements about the earthly Jesus. Only rarely during this time has any scholar dared offer such conclusions on the basis of a strict methodology—although many dilettantish books about Jesus have appeared. Little by little, however, this high degree of skepticism has faded or at least weakened, and in more recent times one scholar after the other has published works which either deal with central and important issues concerning the message and work of Jesus or have bluntly presented total pictures—albeit with varying degrees of qualification.

This does not mean that complete agreement exists among different scholars, and even less does it mean that all basic central questions have been solved. A Swedish scholar, Birger Gerhardsson, has expressed himself as follows concerning the contemporary status of research:

> One can not say that there exists any broad consensus about questions dealing with the person and work of the Jesus of history. The specialists express themselves with great caution on these matters. Consequently, the field lies open and free for all of the world's dilettantes, who are not slow in using the situation and writing 'shock books' which claim to reveal the truth about Jesus. This *triste genre* can always count on a public . . . What one wishes for in this climate of research is that all trustworthy research about Jesus should begin—with more clarity than usual—to mark where the parameters of *uncertainty* concerning Jesus of

Nazareth really are. It is obvious to the initiated that the historical truth about Jesus within *certain* limits is beginning to become clear. . . .[2]

My studies in the last decade's Jesus research tend to validate this point of view. A remarkable agreement exists, especially concerning three chief points: (1) Jesus' central message about the "kingdom of God" which was about to come, and his own personal relation to that event; (2) the content of Jesus' ethical proclamation, and (3) important traits in his behavior and relationship to the different streams within his own Jewish milieu. In light of such agreement it certainly becomes necessary to indicate what is historically trustworthy and where the parameters of uncertainty are—lest one all too easily gets the impression that research is in a far more chaotic state than it really is. Unless the public, which currently possesses a strong interest in the figure of Jesus, is given clear information, the crowds of those who willingly fantasize will be encouraged to proclaim their "truths."

It is not so surprising, however, that serious exegetes have not said much about where these limits of uncertainty extend. They are all too taken up with their special research tasks to devote themselves to "overviews" of this kind. They willingly content themselves with accounting for their own interpretations and positions and with indicating where they differ from the points of view of their colleagues. Although in most cases there is only a cautious attempt to indicate these margins of uncertainty, there remain certain works on Jesus in which the authors have not been hesitant to do so. I speak of books which make the daring attempt to present a total picture of Jesus, his message and activity.

Three of the most notable scholars of our time have recently published such books. One is the "grand old man" of British New Testament scholarship, C. H. Dodd. In 1971, as the mature fruit of his lifelong, comprehensive, and solid research, he published a book with the remarkable title *The Founder of Christianity*.[3] A second is the German scholar, Herbert Braun, who is identified with the influential school of Rudolf Bultmann. His major work, which appeared in 1969, is entitled simply *Jesus*.[4] This is also a product of serious, intensive, and insightful research. A chief task for both of these scholars is, quite naturally, to delimit that which can be seen as historically trustworthy from that which cannot—but they proceed in very different ways.

3

Braun draws distinct and sharp limits; at times he is suspected of being categorical. Fundamentally he does not have much use for the term "uncertain." That which is reported in the text of the gospels is either historically correct or it is unhistorical, stemming not from Jesus but from the early church. For Dodd, elements of uncertainty play a totally different role. He is cautious and meticulous, and his presentation often takes on a hypothetical character. One of his most typical formulations is: "It may be so; or, again, it may not."

3   The third person to mention in this context is Joachim Jeremias, one of the great names in German scholarship, who is especially well known for his research on the parables of Jesus. In 1971 he published a broad overview of *Die Verkündigung Jesu* (The Proclamation of Jesus) as the first volume in an intended "New Testament theology."[5] This learned author is always instructive; this is true not least in connection with his study of Jesus, which possesses a rich wealth of detailed analysis.

Overviews summarize results, but the results come from specialized research, from the investigation of many details. This kind of work is the foundation upon which all attempts to provide total pictures must build. Even if such special investigations do not as a rule devote themselves to indicating the "parameters of uncertainty," they must nonetheless repeatedly deal with such issues as they attempt to answer questions such as: what reason exists for accepting just *this* expression in the gospel text as the authentic words of Jesus? or, are there really valid reasons for doubting authenticity in this or that special case?

Any work which attempts to describe the picture of the earthly Jesus provided by contemporary historical-critical research can scarcely be described as one which indexes and evaluates. The actual situation can be illustrated by a figure with three concentric circles of different shading. The color of the innermost circle is light and represents that which is strongly valid from a historical point of view. The second is shadowy, symbolizing the territory of uncertainty where only doubtful and hypothetical answers can be given. The outer circle with its dark color represents questions which—at least in the present situations—are totally unanswerable. The diagram best fulfills its intention if one tones down the boundaries between the different color zones.

Especially interesting are comparisons among the works of scholars who come from different schools and who attack their research from different starting points. If, under these circumstances, the results of the investigations are in evident agreement, our impression of historical trustworthiness is certainly strengthened. In the following chapters I will attempt a comparison of this sort. But first, in order to have the necessary background of the present situation, we must hastily and extremely summarily review the history of Jesus research in the present century.

Jesus Research in the Twentieth Century

To write about the multi-colored yet fascinating Jesus research of the twentieth century is for me, since I began to study theology even before the turn of the century, to write about experienced history. This is true since over the years I have had direct personal contact with many of the scholars who have held leading positions during this century, including, among many others, Harnack, Schweitzer, Bultmann, and Dodd.

At the turn of the century, the "liberal" theology which had appeared during the last part of the nineteenth century dominated. In 1900 Adolf von Harnack published his famous book *What Is Christianity?*[6] which was widely distributed in many languages. This book represented in elegant form the view of nineteenth-century liberalism. Harnack's position as a leading theologian was primarily based on his magisterial exposé of the history of dogma, which appeared in three large volumes. He desired that the critical point of view which marked that great work be applied to the biblical texts. One of the great merits of nineteenth-century liberalism was that it always insisted that the biblical texts should be the object of the same sort of critical research as was applied to all other historical documents. Many a hot controversy, therefore, was waged with those (as they are now called) "fundamentalists" who actually allowed their biblical interpretations to be determined by traditional dogmatics. Such contrasts were the order of the day during the time of my study.

One of Harnack's most characteristic and oft-quoted sentences in *What Is Christianity?* stated: *"The Gospel, as Jesus proclaimed it, has to do with the Father only and not with the Son."*[7] The importance of Jesus, in other words, lay in his proclamation, his "teaching"—the simple and for all times valid teaching whose chief points were God as our Father, the infinite value of the human soul, and the love commandment. The simplicity in this teaching stood, it was held, in sharp opposition to the complicated theology of Paul, whose work became the starting point for the formation of the church's dogma.

In illuminating subsequent developments, attention should be paid to the following points of view which were generally characteristic of Harnack and liberalism. First, they saw no great difficulty in reaching an authentic picture of Jesus. One had strong confidence in the first three (the "Synoptic") gospels' historical trustworthiness, especially that of Mark, the oldest gospel. Second, the eschatological perspective, which is so obvious in the gospels, was interpreted as something totally peripheral and unessential—it could easily be separated from that which was essential and had lasting value in the teachings of Jesus. The optimism of the late nineteenth century concerning "development" colored the interpretation of Jesus' proclamation of the kingdom of God: that kingdom, to the degree which the teaching of Jesus received response, would more and more be realized and fulfilled in the course of history. Third, the distance between the teachings of Jesus and the Old Testament was strongly emphasized. Harnack even went so far as to advocate the exclusion of the Old Testament from the canon of the church.

When Harnack published *What Is Christianity?* biblical research was already moving in totally different directions. For such research it was clear that Harnack's picture of Jesus was starkly modernized, modeled after patterns of thought which were prevalent among the idealistically-oriented humanists of the nineteenth century. But if research rendered *this* picture of Jesus antiquated, as it had so many earlier pictures, the picture still attracted a high degree of public interest with its accessibility and its opposition to dogma, and it exerted a lasting influence on popular views of Jesus evident even in the present time.

Liberalism's Jesus was in large measure cut off from the time and context in which the earthly Jesus lived and worked. In contrast, a research which was oriented towards the history of religions had even during the nineteenth century maintained that the origin and development of Christianity could never be correctly understood if one did not deal with the religious situation, in all its manifold and kaleidoscopic variety, in which Jesus lived. This type of research experienced a

6

rich flowering during the first decades of the new century. Among its characteristic elements was an accentuation of the role which "Hellenism" played—not least in and through worship, the cult.

For actual research concerning Jesus, however, scholarship which directed itself towards the Judaism characteristic of the "intertestamental period"—that is to say, the time between the last writings of the Old Testament and the origins of the New Testament writings—had greater importance. Attention was directed to the fact that during that era there were extraordinarily strong eschatological-apocalyptic streams which resonated throughout the entire New Testament; the claim was made that Jesus could never be correctly understood if he was not seen against that background. The foremost representatives for this revolutionary point of view were Johannes Weiss and, most notably, Albert Schweitzer. One usually describes Schweitzer's interpretation of Jesus as "thoroughgoing eschatology," but one could rather perhaps use the expression "thoroughgoing apocalypticism." If eschatology sees existence under the aspect of eternity and has its goal set by God, so an *apocalyptic* eschatology lives in the certainty that "the end of time" is near and that the breakthrough of "the kingdom of God" in power and glory is immediately at hand.

Few works have placed Jesus research before such difficult problems as Schweitzer's *Von Reimarus zu Wrede* (the book was published in 1906, and later editions bore the title *The Quest of the Historical Jesus*).[8] Schweitzer here presented a critical review of research about Jesus from its beginning in the time of the Enlightenment, showing how the pictures that were drawn were time and again determined by the cultural milieu of contemporary situations. In contrast to that kaleidoscope of historical pictures, Schweitzer desired to paint Jesus in the colors of his own time. Thus he presented an apocalyptic Jesus who expected that the kingdom of God which he proclaimed would soon be realized, and who went to his death of his own free will, in order by that act of sacrifice both to hasten the arrival of the kingdom and to shorten the aches and pains of "the end-time." It scarcely needs to be said that Jesus thus became an alien and foreign figure, and that his strangeness was emphasized even more by the fact that the course of history did not correspond to his expectations. The problem of Jesus and apocalypticism has never since that time ceased to occupy

7

research. Schweitzer's picture of Jesus became to him a command to follow in sacrificial service—the consequence was his medical work in the forests of Africa.

Schweitzer's critical review of the long development of changing pictures of Jesus which were conditioned by current times could only encourage skepticism concerning the possibility of a historically trustworthy picture. He himself, however, never suffered from any such skepticism. He was convinced that the apocalyptic Jesus was authentic and that the apocalyptic expressions which the evangelists placed in the mouth of Jesus—in any case in all essential matters—were authentic. The next period of research, that of the so-called school of form criticism, had no such confidence in the text of the gospels.

Before I describe this period, I will touch upon yet another complex of conceptions, alongside the apocalyptic, which played an important role in the intertestamental era, and thus also in the New Testament. This complex has been variously named the "demonic" and the "dualistic"—for my part I prefer the term "antagonistic." This designates a struggle between the power of God and the powers hostile to God, which in a certain way are thought to be gathered and concentrated in the devil (Satan, Beelzebul) as the highest representative of evil.

Biblical research with an orientation towards the history of religion has especially emphasized the significance of this perspective in the New Testament. Thus the historian of religion Nathan Söderblom argued that a "dualistic" perspective is an essential part of the Christian message. This is not a question of "metaphysical" dualism between spirit and matter, but one of an opposition between "God and the devil, between the divine, victorious will of love and radical, inexplicable evil." Söderblom rejects the notion that the gospels and Jesus when they speak of the devil should be only "a black spot from the dark times."[9]

This theme attracted considerable attention. In Scandinavian research, in respect to exegesis, it was perhaps most notable in the work of the Norwegian, Anton Fridrichsen, whose productive career was spent in Sweden.

A German scholar who was intensively fascinated by the "demonic" perspective was Rudolf Otto, best known for his famous work *The Idea of the Holy*.[10] In his book *The Kingdom of God and the Son of*

8

Man,[11] undoubtedly one of this century's great books concerning Jesus, Jesus and the demonic powers are a principal theme. Otto strongly emphasized the difference between John the Baptist and Jesus. In Jesus there was the sense of the "bridegroom." For him the kingdom of God was not simply something which was to come in the future; it was rather at that time something which was presently breaking through. Its power was already operating in unceasing struggle with the demonic powers. To speak of driving out evil spirits with "the finger of God" and to describe "one stronger" who overcomes (Matt. 12:26ff.; Luke 11:17ff.) is to assert that it is God's own power which is functioning—through Jesus as the instrument. In Jesus this power, *dynamis,* is operating, setting free the world which has been made demonic. For Jesus, that which is new is not the demand he places; rather it is the penetrating *Heil-kraft-bereich,* in which those who are weak and heavy laden "find rest for their souls."

Probably no group of scholars has had as deep an influence on Jesus research as the so-called form-critical school. Its first proponent was Martin Dibelius (1883–1947), and its most influential leader has been Rudolf Bultmann. For a long time Bultmann dominated gospel research in Germany; he also has had a more far-reaching international influence than any other single scholar.

Form criticism distinguishes itself in important respects from earlier research into the gospels. Its point of departure is its belief that behind the gospels are to be found primitive literary sources which might to some extent be isolated, and with their help one might possibly reach back to Jesus' own words. Form critics are convinced that behind every written expression there is an oral tradition or series of oral traditions. The primitive material consisted of isolated sayings and small units of material which reveal what Jesus said or did. Form criticism directs itself to uncover this oral tradition and the developments through which it progressed before it became fixed in the present text of the gospels. The different elements of tradition are scrutinized and divided into different categories, such as stylistic forms, *genre, Gattungen,* words (*logia*), accounts, and apophthegms. By comparing how these pericopes or blocks of material came into the Synoptic Gospels one could gain knowledge about the different milieus which stand behind various portions of the gospels—their *Sitz im Leben.*

The object of such form-critical scholarship thus became to uncover the way in which small, individual elements were gathered into larger connecting units; it also enabled observation of how the final editorial decisions which shaped the gospels as wholes were made (redaction criticism).

This mode of New Testament scholarship attests to the fact that the gospels were primarily intended as witnesses of faith. Both the orally transmitted reports and the final text of the gospels were from the beginning intended to serve the young and growing church. There is thus no question of any "objective" writing of history. The picture of Jesus which is drawn here is colored and determined by the early church's faith in Jesus as Christ—the Messiah, the risen and glorified Lord-*Kyrios*.

All of this means, says Bultmann, that there is scarcely any possibility of returning to the earthly Jesus. Nevertheless, a few things about his proclamation can be unearthed—Bultmann himself in his younger years wrote an important work entitled *Jesus and the Word*.[12] That book is, characteristically enough, filled with reservations and question marks. What Bultmann the form critic unearthed in the texts of the gospels was above all a reflection of how the tradition had developed and been formed in the early Christian community—Jesus is only a shadow in the background. The result of this research was enormously successful in illuminating the development of the tradition, but extremely meager in respect to the possibility of knowing anything about the historical Jesus. Bultmann's skepticism was, however, not at all designed to unsettle the life of Christian faith; what seems to be a devastating loss was quickly transformed by him into an important gain. The gain consisted in the insight that Christian faith is not at all built upon the result of critical research, but consists rather in the central *kerygma* of the New Testament, its proclamation of the crucified and risen Lord. Faith is thereby liberated not only from all dependence on critical research with its variations and relativities, but also from all the burdensome and, for contemporary man, inaccessible ballast of legendary and "mythological" material which fills the gospels and determines their reports about Jesus Christ: faith is "demythologized."

We encounter something which seems very familiar when Bultmann concentrates all that is essential upon the *kerygma* of the crucified and risen Christ. We recognize the formula from the Pauline letters. But the point of view which is concealed behind Bultmann's formula does not have much to do either with Paul or traditional theology; on the contrary, it is dependent chiefly upon existential philosophy. The meaning of the cross lies in its call to decision, in its demand for "man's death to the world." The resurrection, which according to Bultmann belongs to the world of mythology, symbolizes liberation to an "authentic" life which is created in and through this death to the world.

Whatever one might say about the theological constructions of Bultmann—and our intention is neither fully to present nor to evaluate those constructions—it must unhesitatingly be acknowledged that the work of exegetical research which he and the school he represents undertook has clearly marked a turning point in the history of gospel research. Two factors are important: the uncovering of the difficulties which are encountered in all attempts to reach back to the authentic Jesus, and the important contribution of form criticism to the clarification of the formation of the tradition which led forward to the final fixation of the text of the gospels.

Yet, naturally, all the results of form-critical research are not to be accepted without question. A great amount of international attention has been paid to these results, and they have been discussed in lively fashion both in Europe and America. Appreciation and criticism are often joined together. Objections concern, above all, the balance between the Jesus of history and the continuing growth of tradition within the young church. It is, one might say, correct that the gospels are documents of faith, filled with the church's faith in Christ; that the material of the tradition was chosen with an eye towards the situation of the church; that the reports about Jesus were stylized, embroidered, and interpreted, even reinterpreted, by the different evangelists, each in his own individual way; that additional material has been added during the course of the process, and so forth. But to the extent which Jesus has been made merely into a shadowy image, and the creative power attributed to the anonymous bearers of the tradition, there are strong reasons to call the trustworthiness of the form-critical construction into question. Research has, so to speak, shown its weak side. The point of view which has so roughly put Jesus aside has not been maintained, even within the ranks of form criticism.

11

After 1960

For a long time after the rise of form criticism, few scholarly works concerning Jesus were written. Scholars had become frightened of undertaking such research. They took for granted that it would not pay and that one would lose academic status if one undertook such a task. But little by little the pressure eased. In the 1950s, books about Jesus began to be published again, both by scholars who were counted within the Bultmannian school and by others. Since the beginning of the 1960s, direct research concerning Jesus has come to be an unavoidable and stimulating task for New Testament scholarship. Concentration on this special area of research has been stimulated by a new consciousness that biblical scholarship, when all is said and done, has scarcely any more important task than precisely this one. This is not simply a special field of Christian interest, but a field which has the highest degree of basic historical and humanistic interest.

If literature about Jesus is now experiencing prosperity, we are justified in assuming that scholarship has something definite and essential to say about his preaching and work. Yet recent research has clearly not become less critical, nor does research claim definite answers to all of the relevant questions. On the contrary, critical attention has been sharpened and methodical resources have been developed and refined. As far as answers are concerned, we find in current literature about Jesus a whole range of different positions: historical certainty, probability, possibility, doubtfulness, unattainability.

It can scarcely be contested that research concerning Jesus now has greater possibilities at its disposal than it had earlier and that it has thus entered into a new phase. A series of circumstances has contributed to this. Behind it all lie decades of intensive research, which in the most minute detail has investigated everything which has had and might have importance for an understanding of the gospels. One can without question say that no document in all world literature has been subjected to such careful investigation as the gospels—from all possible points of view—geographical, ethnic, political, social, linguistic, ethical, religious.

It may be appropriate in this context to give some examples of how recent research has corrected certain presuppositions upon which earlier interpretations of Jesus were based. Harnack suggested that the Old Testament should be excluded from the canonical writings of the church—an indication that at root he saw "the essence of Christianity" from the point of view of a fundamental contrast. It has now become quite clear that the New Testament's relationship to the Old is most intimate. Similarly, the history of religions school presupposed that the growing church's meaningful contact with Hellenism took place when the Christian mission proceeded into the Graeco-Roman world. Yet in reality, Judaism in Palestine, in its own land, had ever since the time of Alexander the Great been in contact with Hellenistic philosophy and religion, and Greek was a chief language—the great language of culture—alongside the vernacular tongue of the people. The continued development of research into the gospels and into the intertestamental situation in Palestine has given a far more nuanced picture than earlier generations of scholars possessed.

Among the most important things which have happened in recent years is the widely-known discovery of "new" documents, chiefly at Qumran, which have given a reasonably clear picture of the "Essene sect" which existed there during the time of Jesus. The possibility of more closely determining the relationship of Jesus to different movements and streams within the Judaism of his time has thus been considerably increased. One thing after another has given us a clearer insight than we previously possessed concerning the milieu where Jesus grew up and worked.

The thesis of form criticism that the gospels are documents of faith, colored by the early church's attachments to Christ, was the point of departure for that movement's thorough investigation of the developments which led to the final texts of the gospels. That thesis is and remains irrefutable. Yet this attitude toward the gospels does not necessarily lead to a disavowal of the Jesus tradition. There are possibilities of complementing this thesis with other attitudes towards the growth of tradition. When Bultmann, for example, in his interpretation of Christianity, counts only the cross as historical fact, the picture of the crucified one is dispatched to the kingdom of shadows and the cross is thus placed in a vacuum; or, to change the metaphor, it sways in the wind. It is crucial to emphasize that the form critics have not remained in a state of such extreme skepticism. The school has not only been corrected, but has also corrected itself; one of its more outstanding proponents, Herbert Braun, will soon convince us of this.

The confession of the church in "Jesus the Lord" (*Kyrios Iesous*)

13

attests to the fact that primitive faith in Christ did not swallow up the earthly Jesus. In his untranslated work *Das Kerygma und der irdische Jesus*,[13] Jürgen Roloff has through a great amount of detailed textual analysis shown that the majority of the New Testament accounts of Jesus have preserved *distance* between him and the early church's *Kyrios*. The witness to faith—the *kerygma*—was not disinterested in what Jesus did and said during the days of his life. Any dichotomy concerning *either* the witness of faith *or* historical facticity is without rhyme or reason. For the early church Jesus was not merely an anonymous rallying point for all sorts of views produced by the growing community. The gospels are certainly determined by the faith of the church, but at the same time they strenuously labor to understand what actually happened. There is certainly no proof that particular accounts in the gospels authentically reproduce what Jesus said or did. Yet Roloff's assertion concerning the distance in the gospels between the Jesus of history and the glorified *Kyrios* strengthens the view that the gospels contain historically valid information about Jesus.

Something similar can also be said about the contributions to tradition criticism which have come from Sweden through Harald Riesenfeld and Birger Gerhardsson. The principal work is Gerhardsson's book *Memory and Manuscript*,[14] in which he investigates the pedagogical technique in Jewish education at the time of Jesus and finds that memorization was a common method which, especially within the rabbinic schools, had been carefully worked out and used. It does not appear unlikely that such memorization contributed to the oral tradition about Jesus. Investigations of this sort contribute primarily to our knowledge of the milieu in which the tradition about Jesus was shaped. It ought to be observed in this context that many of the expressions which the gospels attribute to Jesus have in their Greek forms preserved a firm structure which might have made memorization easier. In respect to language, it ought also to be observed that essential contributions to scholarship have in recent times been made by linguistic, semantic, and literary investigations of biblical texts, especially the parables of Jesus.

Following this rapid review of the tension-filled history of Jesus research during our century, I shall proceed, in accordance with the purpose of this book, to present what recent historical-critical research has to say about the earthly Jesus. Naturally, that about which there

14

is scholarly difference of opinion must be accounted for. Since, how-ever, I claim no direct expertise in exegesis, and since I do not trust my own judgments about exegetical questions which are in dispute, I will in the chapters ahead content myself with registering varying points of view. It is to be hoped that future research will, at least in certain cases, achieve greater clarity.

Notes

1. "Earthly Jesus" is an expression which has been deliberately chosen for this book, since the somewhat more common "historical Jesus" is a term which developed within the framework of a previous form of scholarship and has subsequently become encumbered with theological polemic.

2. Birger Gerhardsson, *2000 år senare: Om den genuina Kristustron* (Stock-holm: Verbum, 1972), pp. 38–9.

3. C. H. Dodd, *The Founder of Christianity* (New York: Macmillan, and London: Collier-Macmillan, 1970). This somewhat "popular" work is a clear distillation of a lifetime's rigorous and detailed New Testament scholarship.

4. Herbert Braun, *Jesus: Der Mann aus Nazareth und seine Zeit* (Stuttgart: Kreuz, 1969).

5. Joachim Jeremias, *New Testament Theology: The Proclamation of Jesus,* trans. John Bowden (New York: Scribner's, and London: SCM, 1971).

6. Adolf Harnack, *What Is Christianity?* trans. Thomas Bailey Saunders and with an introduction by Rudolf Bultmann (New York: Harper & Brothers, 1957). This book originally appeared in 1900 as *Das Wesen des Chris-tentums.*

7. Ibid., p. 144 (Harnack's italics).

8. Albert Schweitzer, *The Quest of the Historical Jesus: A Critical Study of Its Progress from Reimarus to Wrede,* trans. W. Montgomery and with an introduction by James M. Robinson (New York: Macmillan, 1968). The German original, *Von Reimarus zu Wrede,* first appeared in 1906.

9. Nathan Söderblom, *The Nature of Revelation,* trans. Frederic E. Pamp, ed. and with an introduction by Edgar M. Carlson (Philadelphia: Fortress, 1966), p. 76.

10. Rudolf Otto, *The Idea of the Holy: An Inquiry into the Non-Rational Factor in the Idea of the Divine and its Relation to the Rational,* 2d ed., trans. John W. Harvey (New York and London: Oxford University Press, 1950). This book originally appeared in 1917 as *Das Heilige.*

11. Rudolf Otto, *The Kingdom of God and the Son of Man,* trans. Floyd V. Filson and Bertram Lee-Woolf (Boston: Starr King, 1957, and London: Lutterworth, 1938). This book originally appeared in 1934 as *Reich Gottes und Menschensohn.*

12. Rudolf Bultmann, *Jesus and the Word,* trans. Louise Pettibone Smith

and Erminie Huntress Lantero (New York: Scribner's, 1958, and London: Fontana, 1960). The German original was published in 1926.

13. Jürgen Roloff, *Das Kerygma und der irdische Jesus: historische Motive in den Erzählungen der Evangelien* (Göttingen: Vandenhoeck & Ruprecht, 1970).

14. Birger Gerhardsson, *Memory and Manuscript: Oral Tradition and Written Transmission in Rabbinic Judaism and Early Christianity* (Lund: Gleerups, 1961; 2d ed. 1964). See also Riesenfeld's celebrated essay "The Gospel Tradition and Its Beginnings" in Harald Riesenfeld, *The Gospel Tradition* (Philadelphia: Fortress, 1970), pp. 1–29.

TWO ANGLES OF APPROACH

Contrast to the Judaic Heritage

It is obvious that all Jesus research must attempt to determine what was unique for Jesus. I wish to begin my review by juxtaposing two different "angles of approach"—two different ways of questioning the material at hand. One approach is represented by the scholar Herbert Braun, who has proceeded from the form-critical approach typified in his *Jesus*. In his work one question which returns time and again concerns the identity of that which is "non-Judaic"; a principal interest in his work is, in other words, to determine that which separates Jesus from that which is Judaic. As representatives for a second angle of approach we choose W. D. Davies and Birger Gerhardsson. Both of these scholars are concerned about the continuity between Jesus and the heritage of Judaism, and chiefly about the continuity between Jesus and the Old Testament. A book by Davies which is of special interest is *The Sermon on the Mount*, which in turn is based on a more major and technical work, *The Setting of the Sermon on the Mount*.[1] Gerhardsson has published a discussion of the ethical message of the Gospel of Matthew in the Swedish volume *Etik och kristen tro*.[2] In a series of studies of this gospel he has depicted "Matthew" as a learned and independent interpreter of the Jesus tradition. The evangelist's interpretation, which was carried through with extraordinarily con-sistent logic, has certainly been made obscure by the final "redactor," but it is nonetheless thoroughly clear. In Gerhardsson's interpretation, "Matthew" comes to take a place alongside Paul and John.

It is obviously of great interest to see to what extent common results can be achieved through these two different angles of approach. I shall begin by giving a relatively detailed resumé of Braun's *Jesus*. When, in contrast to the original objective of form criticism, Braun seeks in this book to present a historically trustworthy picture of the earthly Jesus, we receive a valuable insight into the way a scholar works when he starts at the point of form criticism.

Braun's investigation is bound to the first three gospels, the "Synoptics"—the Gospel of John being left aside. This decision is motivated both by the language and the contents of the Fourth Gospel. The Jesus of history could not have spoken *both* as he did in the Synoptic Gospels and as he did in John—and he did *not* speak as he did in the Fourth Gospel. The language of the Synoptics has its origin in Jesus' contemporary Jewish milieu; the long Johannine monologues with their unnuanced, monotonous polemics against the "Jews" comes, according to Braun, from a Hellenistic background. The faith in Christ which is proclaimed in the Fourth Gospel was formed by the evangelist and the circle within which he worked. The first three gospels are also confessional documents with the Easter faith as presupposition, yet each of them presents the Jesus tradition in its own characteristic way. When the different gospels report one and the same thing—an act performed by Jesus or a word which he spoke—it is often presented with variations which express different tendencies.

Under such circumstances is it possible to discern criteria for distinguishing between "authentic" and "inauthentic" words of Jesus? Braun's answer is that historical-critical research has developed a useful method, but that with this method one still cannot arrive at any binding proof; as in historical research in general, one can rather arrive only at different degrees of probability. Consequently it is easier to determine that which cannot be authentic than it is to be certain about that which is authentic.

Language can serve as a criterion only in the rare cases when it does not have a Judaic character. When at times it reveals a Hellenistic influence, the saying in question can hardly be authentic—as an example, Braun refers to Matthew 11:27, which reads ". . . no one knows the Son except the Father . . ." As a rule, then, the content must function as the criterion. If a saying is markedly different from that which is characteristically Jewish, it is an indication that in all probability it stems directly from Jesus himself. An example of such a totally "non-Jewish" expression is Jesus' word about love to the enemy (Matthew 5:44). For anyone familiar with the Judaism of Jesus' time, it is comparatively easy to make decisions of this sort. But this, certainly, does not prevent one from deciding that expressions which are Jewish in character can be authentic. If, on the contrary, an evangelist ascribes to Jesus words which have a clearly Jewish character but which simultaneously contradict expressions which in all probability are authentic, then the Judaized expressions must be acknowledged as inauthentic—as, for example, when Jesus, according to Matthew, says that not a dot will pass from the law until all is accomplished (5:17–19). This is in direct opposition to the liberation which Jesus declares in respect to individual ordinances of "the law."

Braun does not hide the fact that such an analysis of the words of Jesus rests, to a certain extent, on precarious ground. On one hand, a total view of Jesus' proclamation should be founded upon observations concerning individual utterances; on the other hand, this same total view should be a criterion for the authenticity of the individual sayings. Yet at the same time he firmly rejects the point of view that when a scholar takes a position he should only be out to ventilate his subjective attitudes and sympathies. In reality true scholarship is a work of purely factual interest which must be carried out with sober balancing and great sensibility.

It is not possible, however, to write a biography of Jesus. The tradition about Jesus as given in the gospels has as its background the faith in Christ of the developing primitive church, and it is strongly colored by that faith. From this faith come the titles "Messiah" and "Son of man." Jesus "certainly" never demanded any use of these titles of honor by those who listened to him. The oldest formulation of the text, "the Son of man who shall come in the glory of the Father" (Mark 8:38), refers to a person totally other than Jesus himself.

Concerning the remarkable deeds of Jesus—his "miracles"—Braun refers to the fact that in the worlds of antiquity, both Judaic and Hellenistic, the ability to perform miracles was attributed to pious and God-fearing persons and even to prominent men of power—miracles of healing and natural miracles. Braun himself will not "in rationalistic bluntness" contest anything which has been reported, especially concerning the miracles of healing. On the other hand, he says that he is not prepared to see actual events in the natural miracles—"in any case not in the manner in which these miracles are described in the text." That Jesus healed the sick, which according to the understanding of that time was described as the driving out of demons, is "highly probable." A certain development in the tradition can here

19

be seen. Mark especially describes Jesus' method as "half medicinal, half magical"; he can use saliva as medicine (8:23), and healing power can proceed physically from Jesus' own body, such as in the case of the woman with the flow of blood which had lasted for twelve years (5:27–34). Matthew cannot tolerate such expressions—according to him, Jesus drives out the demons of sickness "with a word" (8:16).

The history of the Passion has, according to Braun, been stylized in a "Christian" context, the historical foundation in many cases seemingly uncertain. The Hellenistic sacramental element in the report on the last supper is foreign to the Palestinian context, and appears to have its background in the Communion celebrations of the Hellenistic-Christian congregations. The historicity of the scene in Gethsemane must also be questioned—who was the witness? The same also pertains to the events in the Jewish court. The hearing before Pilate is similarly stylized in a Christian manner. One never gets any true clarification of the reason for the judgment on Jesus. Braun also calls into question the historicity of Jesus' words from the cross. In Luke these words have a triumphal character which reaches a later climax in John. Regarding the cries of dereliction in Matthew and Mark, Braun expresses his reservations and suggests that here we are dealing with the question of a quotation from the Psalter; he concludes that the oldest tradition knew only a wordless cry (Mark 15:37). Finally, he doubts that there has even been a historical core for the reports concerning the grave and Jesus' burial. The motivations in which the formation of the tradition of the Passion text is rooted are, according to Braun, clear: that Jesus was seen as a martyr and an example for the faithful; the tendency to sharpen the guilt of the Jews and minimize that of the Roman authorities (especially in Luke); the placement of the Lord's supper immediately before the death of Jesus— "Apart from this, the interpretation of Jesus' death as a 'death for sin' (*Sühnetod*) played no role in the history of the Passion."[3]

The question of the relationship of Jesus to *contemporary Jewish apocalyptic* has, as we have seen, played a major role in the Jesus research of our century. To Braun it is apparent that Jesus clothed his proclamation concerning the coming "reign of God" in apocalyptic garb. The breakthrough of the kingdom is immediately at hand. Some authentic words of Jesus speak of how this breakthrough is immediately bound to the arrival of the apocalyptic Son of man, which is to happen suddenly and unexpectedly as "the lightning flashes and lights up the sky from one side to the other" (Luke 17:24). The tradition subsequently identified this Son of man with Jesus, and added embellishments to the apocalyptic pattern. In all probability, among the authentic words of Jesus which count on both the realization of the kingdom of God and the pronouncement of judgment upon the contemporary generation belongs the expression that "it shall be required of this generation" that payment shall be made for the evil blood which has been shed throughout the ages (Luke 11:51). In this context belongs also the expectation of Jesus that he shall, apparently soon, drink the wine "new in the Kingdom of God" (Mark 14:25). Simultaneously, however, Braun emphasizes that Jesus did not intend to specify when "the end" would come—that was known "only to the Father." Jesus' actual interest is directed totally toward admonishing serious, conscientious, and responsible decisions in the crisis situation at hand. Thus we also have, for example, the word about building upon the rock, not upon the sand (Matt. 7:24ff.), as well as the critical word in which the people of the time were compared to children sitting in the marketplace, incapable of a clearly affirmative decision (Matt. 11:16–17), together with many other calls to watchfulness and preparedness—sometimes in the form of parables, and sometimes in direct form.

Apocalypticism's expectation of an immediate end must, says Braun, be interpreted as a mistake (*ein Irrtum*). In the New Testament we actually find in part an advancement of the time of the end from the present generation to later generations, and in part a recasting of conceptions which place the arrival of the kingdom of God in the future. In Luke, therefore, the time of salvation has come with the arrival of Jesus (Luke 4:18–21), and in John the "last things" have already come, in and through the ongoing proclamation. In light of such alterations we find ourselves on solid New Testament grounds when we judge the apocalyptic construction to be a "miscalculation." According to Braun, there is, furthermore, no reason to seek to correct this mistake by changing the apocalyptic "end" to some future point in time. Such attempts would, among other things, not be in agreement with Jesus' preaching about the nearness of the kingdom of God, or with his intention to warn men against making their lives invalid (*sich selber zu verfehlen*). "For essential elements of his proclamation retain their validity even if the apocalyptic horizon disappears."[4]

Up until now we have only dealt with Braun's sharply critical attitude toward the gospel texts. Let us now acquaint ourselves with the picture of the earthly Jesus which he finds to be both essential and historically trustworthy.

The conversion or change of attitude preached by Jesus means most precisely an act of will: man's will "is converted" to total obedience to the will of God. Herein, then, lies a "denial" directed primarily towards one's own self, the actual enemy: "Whoever seeks to gain his life will lose it, but whoever loses his life will preserve it" (Luke 17:33). When Matthew speaks of the demand for a higher righteousness than that which lies on the common Judaic plane, higher than that of "the scribes and pharisees," he has certainly correctly interpreted Jesus' meaning. When Jesus demands conversions and total obedience to the will of God, he is certainly speaking on the Judaic level. But he goes beyond that point when he sets this obedience free from all formal and juridical references, from all systems and fixed codes: he radicalizes the demand for obedience in an extraordinary way by making its realization dependent upon the decision of the individual person.

The most surprising element in Jesus' preaching for conversion, however, is something totally different. Throughout the history of religions there has been a general rule: the more rigorously the demand is formed, the more this leads to a discrimination against people of deviating behavior. In Jesus we find the direct opposite. Braun illustrates this with the account of the pharisee and the publican in the temple, as well as with the parable of the prodigal son. The prayer of the publican is accepted, not that of the pharisee. In the parable, the elder brother shows himself to be actually the lost one. In their own ways, both the pharisee and the elder brother had fulfilled all requirements; their error was that they both interpreted "obedience" as a merit which they could count to their own good. Piety and obedience were for them self-sufficient. Thus obedience to the law—obedience to Torah—became their spiritual pitfall, which showed itself in their hardhearted discrimination against the publican and the younger brother. The idea that obedience to the Torah could be something dangerous did not only lie outside the awareness of contemporary Judaism—it was directly offensive—Jesus was reviled as "a friend of publicans and sinners" and answered in a totally non-Jewish fashion by presenting a child as the example: "Whoever does not receive the Kingdom of God like a child shall not enter it" (Mark 10:15). According to Braun, this expression means that a child receives a gift immediately, without any calculation. In the same manner Jesus' preaching about conversion manifests itself in "a double fundamental chord": a radical demand and a radical, unmerited gift.

Jesus' attitude to the cult. In the gospels, those who most correctly observe the ritual laws concerning purity but at the same time neglect "the most essential part of the law" are often severely criticized. Such criticism undoubtedly stems from Jesus himself. Yet Jesus nevertheless here also remains on the Judaic level, a follower of the prophets. The same sort of criticism was also found in contemporary Judaism, not least in the strict Qumran sect. But while this sect attempted to sharpen the regulations concerning purity, Jesus' concern was totally different: "there is nothing outside a man which by going into him can defile him; but the things which come out of a man are what defile him" (Mark 7:15). Such a radical position stood in opposition not only to contemporary Judaism, but to the laws of purification which were laid down in the Old Testament. This indifferent attitude of Jesus to the laws of purification seemed highly shocking. It was also, in different ways, softened and modified in the tradition which was later developed by the gospel text.

The same relation between an original radicalism in Jesus and a subsequent softening in the tradition occurs with regard to the proper observance of the Sabbath. When Jesus healed the sick on the Sabbath and thereby violated existing laws, he did so regardless of whether his action could be defended by any casuistic course of reasoning. His radicalism was clearly expressed in the words: "The Sabbath was made for man, not man for the Sabbath" (Mark 2:27). With this he declared, in cutting opposition to Jewish thought, that the Sabbath with its many rules was not a religious end in itself and was not intended to serve God. It is characteristic that, in different ways, subsequent tradition modified the radicalism of Jesus. For example, Jesus' behavior was defended by a reference to the fact that even King David violated

23

the rules of the Sabbath (Mark 2:25–26; Luke 6:3–4) and that the priests did likewise. Yet more important was the defense which claimed that Jesus could violate these rules precisely because as Messiah and Son of man he was lord over the Sabbath (Mark 2:28; Matt. 12:6).

Concerning Jesus' attitude to the temple cults and the temple, the texts do not present any simple point of view. The account of the cleansing of the temple seems to be grounded in history. There does not appear in this case to have been any fundamental criticism of the temple cult; it is more likely that we are dealing with a somewhat cautious attitude toward worship by sacrifice.

When Jesus appears indifferent to the regulations concerning cultic observance, he stands in opposition not only to the Judaism of his time but also to a number of Old Testament rules. But he was no iconoclast, either in relation to the temple or to the role of the priests. What was essential for him was that persons should be truly obedient to God and that there should be no opportunity for hiding behind formal ritualism.

Again, when it concerns *legal questions of religion* we find the same pattern: Jesus was radically disinterested, but the tradition modifies his radicalism. Cultic rites and religious law were intimately related in Judaism—the law was at root always religiously oriented. This religious legalism was strange to Jesus. When he indicated that the child was the model for entrance into the kingdom of God, "the juridical distinctions became uninteresting." In rejecting the thought that those who had been victims of Pilate, as well as those who had been accidentally killed when the tower of Siloam fell, were more sinful than all others and were therefore justly punished, his totally un-Jewish attitude "must have been an embarrassment for those who represented the law."[5]

The fact that Jesus' references to the law were often pointed and subtle has nothing whatsoever to do with casuistry. If it is said that one should forgive "seventy times seven" (Matt. 18:22), it does not follow that one should refuse forgiveness the four-hundred-and-ninety-first time. Jesus spreads his sarcasm when hairs are split as to when an oath should be binding (Matt. 3:16–19)—in the following two verses, however, one meets the reasonable attitude characteristic of the primitive church. The same sarcasm reappears when Jesus scolds those who stress the proper tithing of herbs but neglect the weightier matters of the law (Matt. 23:23).

The difference between the non-casuistical instruction of Jesus and the subsequent tradition may be illustrated by several examples. Jesus flatly forbids that one should nurse anger against his brother; the tradition complements this in the same verse by drawing distinctions between different words of abuse (Matt. 5:22). Jesus forbids swearing (Matt. 5:34a); the tradition indicated that an oath, sworn in the name of the Lord, may not be replaced with other formulations (Matt. 5:34b–36). Jesus gives a simple hint for forgiving one's erring brother (Luke 17:3); Matthew gives detailed regulations as to how such a case should be handled in different instances (18:15–17). In totally un-Jewish fashion, Jesus forbids divorce; the tradition modifies this by reference to Jewish praxis. Concerning this command Braun writes that it was intended to protect the woman, who otherwise was totally without rights—in Jesus there was no discrimination against women. These examples—Braun provides others—show how religious law takes its own shape within the Jesus tradition.

Within the Judaism of Jesus' time there was no uniform attitude to property. There was an awareness of the dangers of wealth, but at the same time there was great appreciation for the ownership of property. In the "handbook" of the Qumran sect there are prescriptions against private property; novices were required to hand over their property to the community since it was considered a danger to their spiritual life. Jesus stood nearer to the Qumran view of property than to that of official Judaism. Jesus calls the poor blessed, saying to them "yours is the Kingdom of God" (Luke 6:20). In Matthew the formula "the poor in spirit" (5:3) hides the fact that Jesus was concerned with a question of social poverty. Wealth is dangerous: "How hard it will be for those who have riches to enter the kingdom of God!" (Mark 10:23). But on the other hand, he finds followers not only among the poor and the socially ostracized. "Publicans and sinners" do not belong to this category; they belong to the religiously ostracized.

Jesus had a critical attitude toward property, as does much of the subsequent tradition, but he did not set forth general demands that property must be relinquished. His word to the rich young ruler that "You lack one thing: go and sell everything that you possess and give it to the poor" is a special case, a "pedagogical" demand for a special occasion. Among Jesus' followers were some who owned property: for example, Mary and Martha, Levi, and Peter, who owned a house. In one parable a woman was not scolded for her joy at rediscovering a coin (Luke 15:9–10). The legend of the woman who anointed Jesus with pure and costly nard (Mark 14:3–7) demonstrates no ascetic tendencies. Part of the tradition of the primitive church, especially in Luke, nevertheless takes a sharply negative attitude towards possessions. In Matthew Jesus warns against collecting earthly treasures and urges that one concentrate on heavenly wealth; Luke goes a step further: "Sell your possessions and give alms" (Luke 12:33). In his gospel the rich man precisely because he was rich must endure the tortures of hell. Only in Luke are riches and possessions as such considered to be "unjust." In the Acts of the Apostles an idealized picture is provided of how the primitive community possessed everything in common. It can be authenticated that this purely negative view of property does not go back to Jesus himself.

Love to the neighbor. The word "neighbor" is mentioned only rarely in the gospels, and the word "love" in relationship to one's neighbor is mentioned only very occasionally, except in direct reference to the Old Testament commandment to love God and one's neighbor. This does not mean, however, that this concern plays a subordinate role— on the contrary, it is a principal theme in the proclamation of Jesus. It has in fact, already, shown itself in what has been discussed concerning the relationship of Jesus to the cult, religious law, marriage, and property.

Among the expressions concerning the neighbor which the gospels attribute to Jesus, Braun distinguishes three categories: (1) those which have direct connections with previous or contemporary Judaism; (2) those which supersede contemporary tendencies and have an affinity with more radical trends, especially within the Qumran sect; (3) those in which Jesus surpasses all other demands and sets forth something totally unique.

It would be a digression to review all of Braun's research in this area. Suffice it to say that in the first category belong a great many rules of behavior, as, for example, the "golden rule" (Matt. 7:12), which even in its positive form is to be found within the Jewish tradition; words against anger, words about reconciliation with one's adversary before going to court, the demand for mildness, humility, self-denial, the warning against seeking places of honor, the words about the greatness of service, and the demand that one care for the poor and ill. Among such expressions can be found authentic words of Jesus, but most often a subsequently expanded tradition is found, which appears especially in connection with the characteristically Jewish idea of reward—although, however, one can on occasion find that the tradition has not totally diverged from the way in which Jesus broke down the Jewish code of reward.

Some instances in which Braun finds the words of Jesus somewhat related to the rigorous demands of the Qumran sect have already been mentioned: the requirement that religious duties in respect to the temple and the priesthood not take priority over the care of the neighbor, the requirement for effective economic support of the poverty-stricken, and the requirement of pastoral care for the erring brother. The detailed prescriptions with which Matthew subsequently expands this last demand (18:15–17) coincide nearly verbally with the rules of Qumran.

In the third category, which includes demands unique to Jesus, belong the radical prohibition against judgment (Matt. 7:1) and the prohibition against retribution and self-defense—the saying about turning the other cheek, the saying about the coat and the cloak, and the saying about going two miles in the service of another person when one has been required to go only one mile (Matt. 5:39–42). Jewish texts speak about willingness to render service up to a point; Jesus' sharpened words dissolve all such limits. For him there must be willingness to serve without restrictions. Jewish texts, furthermore, occasionally forbid hatred against another human being and demand that evil be repaid with good; but to hate is still relatively permissible in the case of the rabbis. In the "handbook" of Qumran, love is demanded towards one's friends in faith, but hatred is required toward outsiders. Jesus commands love towards one's enemies, including religious enemies, and in so doing remarkably restructures the concept of the neighbor.

Everything that Jesus says concerning one's relationship to his neighbor is determined by the demand that one should be of help to him. Nothing may be allowed to stand in the way of care for the neighbor.

His bitter criticism of the scribes and pharisees belongs in this context: "They bind heavy burdens, hard to bear, and lay them on men's shoulders" (Matt. 23:4); they "shut the Kingdom of Heaven against men: for you neither enter yourselves, nor allow those who enter to go in" (Matt. 23:13). So-called religious duties have no priority here: neither rules for the Sabbath, nor the so-called Corban, which sets the promise of a gift to the temple above the care of one's parents (Mark 7:9–13). Jesus' view concerning relationships to one's neighbor has left its imprint in the tradition, as exemplified in the great vision of the final judgment (Matt. 25:31–46) in which the verdict depends upon whether or not one has served Jesus by caring for those in need: "one of the least of these." Jesus is the judge of the world, not in that he requires honor for his own sake, but rather in that his will is to be done through care for the needy.

Forgiveness is a word mentioned in Jewish contexts. The one who prays is to forgive in order that he himself might be forgiven by God— as in the first petition of the Lord's Prayer. The radical demand of Jesus unconditionally questions whether it is possible to fulfill that command. The disciples ask: "Then who can be saved?" The answer is given: "With men it is impossible, but not with God" (Mark 10:26–7). It is a question of *radical grace*. Jesus preaches about this—without using the term itself—mostly in the parables. The radical demand and the radical grace are at times placed nakedly alongside each other: man has only to receive with empty hands. In other instances, command and grace are bound together in such a way that true obedience grows from the gift which is received.

A series of parables, such as the laborers in the vineyard and the prodigal son, demonstrates how Judaism's traditional scheme of reward is broken down. The gift is presented without regard to merits; grace is sovereign. The laborers who grumble bespeak that jealousy which looks upon the goodness of the giver with evil eyes. The prodigal son receives a totally undeserved grace; the mistake of the older brother was that he counted the whole time on a reward, and thus he became the lost son, bitter towards his father and brother. The story of the sinful woman in the house of Simon (Luke 7:36–50) demonstrates how the gift of grace produces thanksgiving and love. The words of the text which are marked by tradition—"her sins, which are many, are forgiven, for she loved much"—are reminiscent of the scheme "merit-grace" but are corrected by the narrative as a whole.

A chief question now becomes whether or not Jesus merely proclaimed this sovereign grace or whether "he personally belongs to this proclamation" as an inescapable part of it. Braun here takes up exactly the same question which Harnack raised for his time in *What Is Christianity?* Harnack answered negatively; Braun gives the opposite answer.

An investigation of the Synoptic texts in relation to this question forces one, says Braun, to disregard that which the tradition, on the grounds of the Easter faith, has added concerning Jesus as the Messiah and his atoning death. Nor can one begin by interpreting a parable as though Jesus were unquestioningly in the picture: for example, as though he were the good Samaritan. Tradition has developed in this direction, as evidenced by the use of the formula "for my sake" as a motivation for works of love. Nevertheless, there are texts which substantiate Braun's position. Even though accounts of Jesus' association with "sinners and publicans" have been schematized by the tradition, the question of whether Jesus really acted thus must unconditionally be answered in the positive. The words of abuse directed towards him—a glutton and drinker, the friend of publicans and sinners—undoubtedly bear witness to how by his actions he carried his proclamation into effect. His behavior uncontestably belongs with his proclamation. "It must be historically correct that in concrete situations 'on earth' (Mark 2:10) he declared to persons the forgiveness of their sins." He not only preached "grace," but also transformed his message into action.[6]

The *authority* of Jesus depends, it is often said, upon the fact that he was "the Son of God." But authority in the basic sense of the word, says Braun, can only be gained inwardly. Such was the case with the authority won by Jesus. His proclamation and acts won the heart and the conscience: "He taught them as one who had authority" (Matt. 7:29). In the same manner Jesus could also win trust. Certainly it is not now a matter of agreeing *in blanco* with all that he said—for example, with his expectation of the imminent end. The issue is that of "an authority in dialogue" which results in a positive response to that which is unconditionally convincing.

Braun gives a resumé of how the interpretation of Jesus' authority is developed and formed within the framework of the New Testament: Jesus is given a series of titles of honor, and a whole system of conceptions about his life develops. His way went from heaven, from pre-existence as the *Logos*, through the virgin birth to earthly *kenosis* (Philippians 2:7) and then through death, resurrection, and ascension back to his original existence in heaven. "I can understand," writes Braun, "that one used these conceptions in order to explain the authority of Jesus, and I am in agreement with these early Christian formulations insofar as Jesus in word and deed at definite and important points has become the authority also for me." Such a confession may, in the opinion of many, be all too little; "dogmatic correctness" is demanded if it is not to conflict with the New Testament. That book, however, is itself well aware of the spiritual danger which arises when one does not distinguish between such correctness—"Lord, Lord"—and the authority by which Jesus in word and deed quite concretely conquers man.[7]

Mark reports that Jesus was once questioned concerning the authority by which he acted (11:27–33). Jesus answers with a counterquestion: "Was the baptism of John from heaven or from men?" One could conclude that this was evasive, but according to Braun it is the precise answer to the question of the chief priests, the scribes, and the elders—although in indirect form. Jesus' answer is: *from God.* Why did he not give a direct answer? Precisely because he and his adversaries conceive of God in totally different ways. When Jesus says "God," he thinks of radical demand and total grace. Whoever responds positively to this testifies that the authority of Jesus comes from God: God is, so to speak, implicated in this positive response. When his adversaries do not give such an answer, Jesus cannot openly say that his authority comes from God without being misunderstood by them.[8] Jesus' understanding of God involves an extraordinary changing of the horizon. For the Judaism of his time God was an entity unto himself; he was to be served in the cult according to certain fixed Sabbath regulations. For Jesus, on the contrary, the Sabbath is for the sake of man, and to serve God is to serve men in their need.

The Synoptic Gospels are dominated by a concern for the meaning of love to the neighbor—love to God is mentioned, with one exception, only when the double commandment is quoted. This obviously does not mean that God disappears from the proclamation of Jesus: everything centers around "the reign of God." The point is that God is not to be loved in "ecstasy" or in ritual observance, but in love's care for the neighbor.

This picture of God in action becomes clear when we pay attention to *how* the grace of God is spoken of, how it is both compared and contrasted with the gifts which are given by human beings. A father is not so unreasonable as to give his son a stone when he asks for bread. A man gets up in the middle of the night in order to give help which has been requested (Luke 11:5–8). The conclusion is: "how much more will your Father who is in heaven give good things to those who ask him?" (Matt. 7:11). Jesus shows what we can expect from the goodness of God. The generous human is but a faint image of the lavish God. Here Jesus comes into the picture as the one who turns himself to the ostracized, the poor, the sinners and the publicans: "In the community which attempts to live on the basis of love of Jesus, man can breathe . . . [and] the poor, impious, and evil person may, unexpectedly, again be called human"—that is, be accepted. This also makes it possible for man to accept himself, as did the prodigal son.[9] Not until this happens have we rightly understood what the grace and forgiveness of God involve.

The word "God" has many meanings. Among the contemporaries of Jesus it *could* mean earning salvation through obedience, and it *could* mean the duty of the pious to hate. For Jesus, all hate gives way to love, and for him God is not an authority before whom man can earn anything. Here, instead, a future and a hope are given to evil persons and to those who live without hope. "Only in the interpretation of the Gospels does the word God have only one meaning."

To many of the problems connected with Braun's interpretation of Jesus I will return. Here I shall limit myself to a few preliminary comments concerning his position.

The radically critical stance which he takes bears witness to his affinity to the form-critical school, but he does not at all share the indifference to Jesus research which originally marked that school. On the contrary, he shows great interest in coming to terms as intimately as possible with the earthly Jesus. Nor does he share the tendency of early form criticism to reduce Jesus in importance and emphasize that which was created by anonymous builders of tradition in the primitive church. It is certainly clear to Braun that the texts of the gospels were not only formed in and of themselves, but also that a great deal of their content stems from the perspective of the faith of the early church. But the composite picture which Braun gives of the proclamation of Jesus makes it fully clear that according to him the originality stems from Jesus himself. Finally, it is not insignificant that Braun asserts with certainty that Jesus himself belongs to the gospel which he proclaims, that he is the bearer of the gospel and manifests it in deeds—this in sharp contrast to earlier nineteenth-century "liberalism" as well as to the older form-critical view.

Continuity with the Judaic Heritage

Having acquainted ourselves with the argument typified by Braun, at the center of which stands the question of the "non-Jewish," we turn now to Davies and Gerhardsson to see how the argument proceeds when one stresses the continuity between Jesus and the heritage from Israel. Neither of these has written a book dealing directly with the question of Jesus himself. Their writings which shall be dealt with here are mainly concerned with the Gospel of Matthew and, more specifically, with the ethical message of that gospel. Neither has in detail handled the problem of the relation of Jesus to the text of the gospel, but nonetheless, their presentation of the relation of Matthew to the texts provides considerable insight into what Jesus himself might have taught.

Davies and Gerhardsson each have a marked profile. When they are placed here side by side, it is chiefly because of the fact that the word "Think not that I have come to abolish the law and the prophets; I have come not to abolish them but to fulfill them" (Matt. 5:17) is a common theme. This verse is cited by both as an expression which gives direction to Jesus' own view of his relationship first to "the law" and also to the Old Testament in general. A certain observable point of contact between the two is also to be found in their interpretation of Matthew as a scribe whose theology was worked out with great consistency. Gerhardsson is one who expresses himself most definitely about this:

> No book in the New Testament is marked by such learning and consistency as Matthew's Gospel. The material has been stylized, the chief lines and the basic pattern have been worked out with a totally different kind of clarity than that which is found in the other Gospels . . . but

> the presentation has simultaneously removed itself more from that which is concretely historical than is the case in the descriptions given by Mark. . . . We are here dealing with *historical interpretation* rather than *historical writing*.[11]

Davies has also pointed out that Matthew is the evangelist who more than any other has placed his personal stamp on the text of his gospel. About his writing he says: "It reveals a meticulous concern in the arrangement of its details and architectonic grandeur in its totality: its different parts are inseparable, like those of a well planned and well built house."[12]

W. D. Davies is British by birth and training but for some time has been pursuing scholarship in the United States. Like other contemporary exegetes he has profited greatly from the research of form criticism, but thanks to his background he has also preserved a critical distance from that school.

Since Davies has such a high estimate of Matthew as a learned, theologically alert scribe, the question of how Matthew himself viewed the compilation and formation of that material which goes under the name of "the Sermon on the Mount," but which is not one connected sermon, is made unconditionally important. It is, says Davies, apparent from the beginning that this compilation, stemming from different sources, has been formed in the interests of the Palestinian church. "The needs of the Church *have* dictated, if not created, much of the form and, probably, some of the contents of the material."[13] Liturgical elements have also crept in—as an example, Davies shows how the form of the Lord's Prayer differs in Matthew and Luke.

What Matthew means with "the Sermon on the Mount" Davies concentrates in two words: "messianic Torah," the Messiah's law. Before we go further into this theme, we shall first pay attention to a few elements in Davies's description of the situation in Palestine when the first gospel came into being, elements which he finds to be essential both for the interpretation of "the Sermon on the Mount" and the Gospel of Matthew as a whole. We must deal here in part with the situation of Judaism at that time, and in part with the relationship of the gospel to the Qumran sect. Jerusalem had fallen, the great portion of the Jewish people had been massacred by the Romans, and others had been carried away into slavery. In this emergency situation in which it appeared that the Jewish people might go under, rabbinism carried out a magnificent work of consolidating and stabilizing Judaism. This happened in a tucked-away place, Jamnia. "A common calendar was established for all Jews . . . a common liturgy was attempted for the Synagogue; the canon of the Old Testament came to be fixed: the rabbinate was given greater significance and, more important still, beginnings were made in fixing the tradition of Jewish law; the Mishnah, the Jewish code of law, began to take shape . . ." Matthew's attempt in the Sermon on the Mount to give a concentrated presentation of Jesus' ethical teachings was done in conscious opposition to the Judaism of Jamnia. "We now suggest that Matthew was conscious of Jamnia as was Jamnia of the new faith, and that the shadow of Jamnia lies over his Gospel . . . Matthew was concerned to set forth a Christian law over against that of Judaism . . ."[14]

Another meaningful circumstance was that Qumran was destroyed and the members of the sect were dispersed, and that, in all likelihood, some of them had become members of the Christian church. It is Davies's opinion that the contact between the church and the sect on the one hand influenced the text of the gospel, and on the other hand led to sharp polemics. In Matthew are found both influences from different sources and polemics against different elements. "Nevertheless, what chiefly led him [Matthew] to concentrate on using the words of Jesus himself, sectarian conventions, and rabbinic forms in the Sermon on the Mount was the desire and the necessity to present the ethic of the New Israel, the Church . . ."[15]

It was the intention of Matthew, therefore, in chapters 5–7, to give a summary of the messianic Torah. When Jesus speaks "on the mountain," the giving of the law on Sinai is used as a prototype. Yet the one who speaks is not simply a new Moses. The prologue of the gospel with its genealogy and birth narrative is intended to show that Jesus' entrance into history introduced a new era and involved a new work of creation, comparable only to the creation of the universe. Jesus is a new Adam and, as the Son of David the King, he is the Messiah. He is Israel, and recapitulates in his life the life of the people of Israel— "Out of Egypt have I called my son" (Hosea 11:1, Matt. 2:15). He is Emmanuel, "God with us," suggesting "the presence of the God who was active in creation and is now, through Jesus, with his people."[16] The epilogue of the gospel is reminiscent of the prologue. Here Jesus also speaks "on the mountain" to his disciples. He speaks as the sovereign: "All authority in heaven and on earth has been given to me" (Matt. 28:18). When he instructs the apostles to make all people his disciples and teaches them to observe all that he commanded, we are referred back particularly to the law which as Messiah he gave in the Sermon on the Mount. Of great importance also in this context is Matthew's account of the transfiguration of Jesus (17:1–8). In all three Synoptic Gospels this account has elements which remind us of how Moses received the law on Mount Sinai. Certain peculiar formations have emphasized the position of Moses in Matthew's version of the transfiguration, and when at the end he allows the voice of God to admonish the people to obey Jesus as the beloved Son of God, "there can be little doubt . . . that this points to Jesus as an ethical teacher, like Moses."[17]

The law proclaimed by the Messiah is intended to regulate life in the church. At the same time Davies emphasizes that this law "is personalized in Jesus in a way in which the Law of Judaism was never personalized in Moses." The Christian life is to be a following after Jesus: "The marks of the life of Jesus are to be traceable in that of his followers . . . the ethical norm for Christians is not only the words but the life also of him who uttered them. The shadow of Jesus' own life is over all the Sermon." For Matthew Jesus is not only a teacher; the title he uses most often is "Lord." Christians are disciples "within the larger context of incorporation in Jesus and worship of him as their Lord. There is a kind of identity between the Matthaean Christian and his Lord which is not unlike the understanding of Christians as being 'in Christ' which we find in Paul."[18]

The law which the Messiah proclaims is, however, according to Matthew, not a "new" law. Mark describes the proclamation of Jesus as a new teaching, but Matthew consistently avoids using the word "new" about the law. The old law of Israel remains. Jesus has not come to abolish but to fulfill. None of the antitheses in the Sermon on the Mount intend to annul—rather, they intend to carry out the demands of the law "to their ultimate meaning," to reveal a deeper meaning for a new era. Also in respect to such critical points as Jesus' position toward Sabbath rules, rules of purification, and the question of divorce, Matthew desires to show that Jesus, even if he is critical of the tradition, does not stand in opposition to the old law but rather fulfills it through his interpretation.

Matthew's treatment of the tradition of Jesus shows, however, how Jesus' "*radical* words begin to take on a *regulatory* character" and how "the confrontation of the words of Jesus with Judaism in Matthew did provide for the possibility of the legal understanding of the words of Jesus . . ."[19] In the Sermon on the Mount, and in other places in his Gospel, Matthew, with the intention of regulating and disciplining, has modeled and modified: as for example, with regard to divorce and the command against nursing anger. Another example concerns the words of Jesus: "Do not judge" (Matt. 7:1). Both the rules about how an erring brother should be treated (18:15–16) and the word about not casting pearls before swine (7:6) abolish with their regulating intent the lack of compromise in the words of Jesus. Matthew has softened the radicalism in the ethics of Jesus—and this has happened in accordance with the fact that within the church "there is constantly going on a process of 'binding and loosing,' of allowing certain things to be done and forbidding other things."[20] This tendency to transform Christianity into something rabbinic is not peculiar to Matthew. It appears also in Paul.

In the last chapter of his book, Davies poses the question which for both him and us is a principal issue: "Has Matthew, by clothing Jesus in the role of the lawgiver and thus rabbinizing him, given to the Lord a garb which falsifies 'the Jesus of history,' that is, Jesus insofar as we can know him as he actually lived? Can we define the relation in which the Christ of the Mount stands to Jesus himself?"[21]

Jesus was, according to Davies, an eschatological figure. This means that his teaching was of a different kind than that of the rabbis. When Jesus proclaims that the kingdom of God is near, it is certain that "the kingdom of God in him is on the way." His hearers did not consist—as did those of the rabbis—only of immediate followers. He spoke to crowds of people and to "sinners and publicans," with whom he freely associated, and the circle of his disciples arose in response to his call to follow him, involving a personal commitment to imitate him.

The study of the law did not involve the same kind of crisis for the rabbis as did the call of Jesus. In the former case it was the study of the Torah which was the real concern—in the latter case, it was Jesus himself. "And it is this personalism also that made of the disciple of Jesus not another rabbi but an apostle."[22] We must, however, not totally deprive Jesus of his relationship to the rabbis. Jesus also had

36

a kind of "school" gathered around him, "not a strictly rabbinic school but yet one that had rabbinic traits." Jesus explained the law and discussed different legal matters with critics who were learned in the Scriptures. Jesus behaved, Davies emphasizes, in a twofold manner: as an eschatological figure, and as a rabbi or ethical teacher. In the course of the history of Jesus research one of these roles has often been emphasized at the cost of the other. Actually, both of these aspects—the eschatological and the ethical—are inseparably bound to one another in Jesus. The gift and the demand cannot be separated from each other.

The question is now that of the relationship between the ethical proclamation of Jesus and the old law. From his dialogues with the scribes and pharisees it is clear that Jesus took the law seriously. He honored the law even when he attacked it. He was critical, as were the Sadducees, of expansions of the law which were found in the precepts of the elders. But Jesus rejected such expansion in order instead to give his own interpretation of the law, and thus his position was totally foreign to the conservative stance of the Sadducees. The pharisees desired to build further on the law to make it relevant to the current situation—Davies calls this attitude liberal. There is much evidence that at the beginning Jesus had a certain sympathy with the pharisees. Yet his conflict with them became the sharpest; the oral tradition which they erected did not correspond to the spirit of the law.

The position of the Qumran sect is described by Davies as radical. In a manner similar to that sect, Jesus came with a call to decision in anticipation of an eschatological final act which was expected in the near future. It is clear that he criticized the sect on the basis of its exclusively closed fellowship and its iron-hard discipline. But his criticism was directed also against that view of the law which led to a demand for love toward the brethren but hatred for those who were outsiders or who did not possess understanding. Against this Jesus said "Love your enemies," and thereby gave God's will a radically different interpretation than did the sect. Davies establishes that "the law and the prophets" in the Old Testament retained their validity for Jesus as expressions of God's will: "There is no complete break in Jesus with the ethical teaching of Judaism." The accounts of Jesus' work have been colored by the fact that they were formed in a time when the church and the synagogue were becoming increasingly separate from each other. Jesus himself seems to have been more moderate in his attitude to the Judaic cult and its pattern of behavior. He went to the synagogue and to the temple festivals, accepting such religious customs as fasting, prayer, and almsgiving. "He came not to destroy. On the other hand, he did come to fulfill." Much in his works shows a sovereign freedom with respect to the law, such as his attitude toward the Sabbath and his handling of the issue of purity and impurity. But, writes Davies, "it is extremely doubtful whether at any point Jesus *specifically* annuls the law. Thus, in discussions on the Sabbath and on divorce he remains within the framework of the Law. At one point only can he be seriously considered to have destroyed the Law, in Mark 7, and on examination even this point is doubtful"[23] (Davies refers to Jesus' expression concerning what is pure and impure). The conclusion is that it was not his *estimate* of the law as an expression of the will of God which separated Jesus from contemporary Judaism, but his interpretation of what God's will, revealed in the law, involved.

In the gospels we encounter Jesus' ethical proclamation in different contexts: judgment, creation, and the law of Israel. Davies stands in opposition to those who hold that the ethic of Jesus was basically determined by an expectation of an imminent end to this era and by an impending judgment, and that his words consequently were valid only for the comparatively short time which remained. "There is," writes Davies, "much in the teaching of Jesus which does not bear this character, but it is clearly applicable to all times." And further, "Even if Jesus did contemplate the End of all things soon, this in itself was not the secret of his illumination."[24]

Creation has a definite place in the proclamation of Jesus. His words about marriage are grounded in the very act of creation; the creator's purpose was indissoluble marriage, "but the law of Moses slipped in later, owing to the hardness of men's hearts, to allow divorce." Jesus' command to love one's enemies is grounded in that which happens in the world of nature: "so that you may be sons of your Father who is in heaven: for he makes his sun rise on the evil and the good, and sends rain on the just and on the unjust" (Matt. 5:45). Such a view of the relationship between the creation and the ethical acts of human beings has its roots in the Old Testament where there exists an inner connection between nature and man: the right life is the "natural" life. But when Jesus anchors his ethical admonitions in the creation, it does not mean that that which is unique in his instruction could be deduced only from the principle of "the created." One of the texts from Qumran also speaks about marriage and the creation in a manner similar to the formulation of Jesus—but this principle did not produce "that moral illumination which we find in Jesus."

When Davies, in conclusion, takes up the problem of Jesus' relationship to the law of his people, he begins with a few words about the much-debated question of the messiahship. He presupposes that Jesus saw himself as the Messiah, and that as such it was necessary for him to come to terms with the law of Israel. That he did so is apparent from the antitheses in the Sermon on the Mount, even if there is scarcely any doubt that the formulations themselves are the work of the evangelist. A starting point for an understanding of Jesus' relationship to the law is to be found in the last antithesis which deals with radical love for the neighbor, an antithesis whose formulation probably goes back to Jesus himself.

"The concept of love is undoubtedly the best summation of the ethical teachings of Jesus." We are accustomed to emphasizing three things as essential to Jesus' interpretation: the inseparable joining of love for God with love for the neighbor, the reduction of all commandments to this double commandment which was thereby given indisputable priority, and the extension of the term "neighbor" to everyone, which thereby made the love commandment universal. All this is true, says Davies. But yet it is more important to pay attention to the way Jesus revealed the elements of the concept of love, *agape*, through "the pure, unlimited, self-giving" which we meet in his own person.[25]

How did Jesus arrive at this deep understanding of the will of God? Davies answers: "He passed beyond all principles he inherited, beyond the light of the Law and Prophet, to what we can only call an intuitive awareness of the will of God in its nakedness." He expressed this awareness in words about the nearness or presence of the kingdom of God, present in his ministry. It was this "that illuminated him—his awareness of the Sovereign Rule of God in and through himself. This meant that whereas for Judaism the Law expressed the will of God, for Jesus his immediate awareness of the will of God became Law." We stand here before "the fundamental mystery of the person of Jesus himself. He himself in his own intuitive awareness of the will of God is the source of the radical ethic."[26]

Thus Davies can answer his own question as to whether or not Matthew, in concentrating on the words of Jesus as a "new Law," has departed from the spirit of Jesus. The answer is both *yes* and *no*:

> Insofar as he (Matthew) thereby recognizes that there is a demand, as well as a gift, at the heart of the Gospel, he remains true to Jesus. But by gathering together the words of Jesus and isolating them, to some extent, and presenting them as a unified collection constituting a 'law' in an external or independent sense, he has made it possible for many to isolate the ethical demand of Jesus from its total setting as a part of the Gospel and thus distorted awareness of that demand.

This was certainly not the intention of Matthew. "We read the Sermon on the Mount in isolation from the grace of Jesus' ministry contrary to his (Matthew's) purpose."

In a few final words Davies sharpens the necessity for preserving an indissoluble connection between grace and the demand. The idea of grace can also be isolated in a fateful way:

> Emphasis on the act of Christ in life, death, and resurrection, central and essential as it is in all the New Testament, is never wholly free from the danger of abstraction from life. It is the penetrating precepts of Jesus that are the astringent protection against any interpretation of that life, death, and resurrection in other than moral terms. In this sense, the words of Jesus are part of the Gospel and Matthew a true interpretation of the Lord's mind: the Gospel is both gift and demand— a demand to be applied.[27]

In the last chapter of Davies' book, we see even more clearly what he has in mind. He raises the question of whether the gulf between different confessions—Protestant and Roman Catholic, Lutheran and Calvinist—might not be bridged in terms of the wholeness of the New Testament. "Certain it is that the Sermon on the Mount in its setting spans the arch of Grace and Law, conjoins demands such as those of "the right strawy Epistle" of James with the Pauline profundities. Its opening, the Beatitudes, recognizes man's infinite need for Grace, his misery; its absolute demand recognizes man's infinite moral possibilities, his grandeur."[28]

Birger Gerhardsson's writings have, during the last decade, been strongly directed to the Gospel of Matthew. Even though he has not written, strictly speaking, a book on Jesus, the person and proclamation of Jesus have nevertheless been the center of all his work.[29]

The question of Jesus' position in relation to the law of Israel is a principal theme in the writing of Gerhardsson, as well as in the work of W. D. Davies. For both it is essential to indicate that Jesus did not come to annul but to fulfill. In Gerhardsson, however, we find a more penetrating and basic treatment of this theme. As we have already seen, he holds "Matthew" in high esteem as a theological writer—a learned evangelist trained in a rabbinical school, working with strict consistency and in a remarkable way setting his own personal stamp on the text of his gospel. His profound familiarity with the spiritual heritage of Israel and his eagerness to maintain a connection with that heritage make especially possible on his part an understanding of Jesus, but at the same time have caused him to modify the radicalism in Jesus' ethical proclamation.

Gerhardsson is critical of the trend in twentieth-century research which views Jesus' proclamation of the kingdom of God in a one-sidedly eschatological manner. The eschatological perspective is certainly important; but if it is made singularly central, one does not give credit to the source of the material. Jesus speaks often of the kingdom of God ("the kingdom of heaven" in Matthew) as something which is and has been: "God has his kingdom and exercises his reign also in the present, even if he has decisive plans for the future." This point of view is especially important for an interpretation of the ethos of Jesus. The eschatological perspective colors the interpretation of "the will of God" but it does not break the continuity with "that which God has previously ordered for his people."

When Gerhardsson analyzes what this continuity entails, he directs his analysis to the covenant faith of Israel concentrated in the *Shema,* with its double command of love to God and love to the neighbor. The text of the *Shema* is from Deuteronomy 6:4ff.: "Hear, O Israel: The Lord our God is one Lord; and you shall love the Lord your God with all your heart, and with all your soul, and with all your might . . ." The word "love" refers more to an attitude than to a feeling; one is to obey God and to be faithful to him, whole-heartedly and undividedly. The scribes whom the pharisees followed had explained the phrase "with all your soul" as meaning "even if he takes your soul"; in other words, that which was demanded was preparedness to sacrifice life rather than to act against the commands of God. "With all your might" was explained as "with all your mammon": that is, with all that you possess.

The pharisees were deeply concerned with emphasizing this inner side of the law, and this was appreciated by Jesus. He listened positively to the scribes who were "not far from the kingdom of God" (Mark 12:34). "There is greater similarity between the scribes and Jesus in respect to ethical instruction than one sees if attention is paid only to the Gospels' criticism of 'hypocrisy.'"

In an extremely provocative way Gerhardsson has sought to show the significance of the triple interpretation of the *Shema* for Matthew's structuring of the gospel texts. The account of the temptations in the wilderness reveals that Jesus fulfilled the different demands made by the *Shema*. The propositions concerning alms, prayer, and fasting (Matt. 6) follow its pattern;[30] similarly, the description of the crucifixion bears witness to how these three demands were actualized at the end—with special emphasis on the sacrifice of "the soul," life. Another indication of this fulfillment is the fact that the parable of the sower (Matt. 13:3–23), which according to Gerhardsson holds a "key position" in the Gospel of Matthew, can be interpreted with reference to the *Shema*: the three cases where the seed does not bear fruit are due to failure to observe the three basic demands in the *Shema*.[31] Gerhardsson emphasizes that the *Shema* also had direct significance for Jesus himself. Doubtless, like all pious Jews, he recited and seriously meditated on this fundamental text of Israel daily. This is strongly reflected in the demands which Jesus placed before those who desired to follow him, but also, and above all, it influenced his own pattern of behavior.

What, then, does "love to God" mean, according to Jesus? A material answer to this question cannot be given if one isolates and cuts off the relationship to God from the relationship to the neighbor. The command to love God and the command to love the neighbor are inseparable. The theme of one's relationship to the neighbor appears, with rich variety, in the gospels, although in contrast, there is very little said directly about love of God. "Sometimes," writes Gerhardsson, "one gets the impression that God's demand is exclusively a demand to care for one's fellow human beings and that the demand concerning a positive relation to the heavenly Father as such belongs to that which can be disposed of." However, nothing would be more incorrect. The command to love God is totally basic, and the command which above everything else is decisive is that the children of the kingdom of God are to do the heavenly Father's will (Matt. 7:21; 12:50). The demands which stem from the *Shema* appear frequently in the gospel. "With all your heart" means wholehearted obedience in contrast to hypocrisy, outward appearances, and cheap observances of piety. The key word "with all your soul" is encountered in the demand that one be prepared to sacrifice without restrictions—that is, if it be required, even to sacrifice life itself: "If any man would come after me, let him deny himself [a parallel expression to 'soul'] and take up his cross and follow me" (Matt. 16:24). "With all your might" is a theme which resounds strongly throughout the gospels, in which one often hears about the proper relationship to mammon, possessions, and power. The most important word of Jesus in this latter regard is "You can not serve God and mammon" (Matt. 6:24). "To the negative side of this theme belong not only warnings against the dangers of wealth, but also warnings against striving after power and glory in the eyes of men, 'status.' "[32]

Such a view of what is involved in love for God has direct consequences for one's relationship to fellow human beings, neighbors. "Obedience towards God expresses itself in a self-giving, generous attitude towards one's neighbor: not to nurse anger against one's brother, not to commit adultery even in one's heart, not to secure advantages by means of oaths or threats, rather to meet evil with good and to include even one's enemies in love and intercession." The two love commandments belong so intimately together that the "first" commandment can be considered fulfilled as soon as the "second" has been fulfilled. In the scene of the last judgment it is clear that mercy which is directed toward the needs of one's fellow human beings is a fulfillment of the will of the heavenly Father.

Through his concentration on the double commandment of love as the basic commandment, Jesus "fulfills" the law. This basic law is given priority above all other commandments. Jesus does not formally abolish the concrete commandments which have been given, but he "trivializes" them: their literal meanings treat all too inadequately what is at stake—the demands which concern one's relation to his neighbor *are made radical.*

Other commandments which deal with ritual and observance *are made light of*: they can be fulfilled without reference to the basic law and in a way which rather prevents than increases care for one's fellow human beings. This is the background to Jesus' severe criticism of the scribes and the pharisees. A reference from Hosea stresses the connection of this with the criticism of the Old Testament prophets: "For I desire steadfast love and not sacrifice" (6:6). In an article concerning Jesus' attitude toward life, Gerhardsson writes that God is, according to Jesus, "not very interested in sacrifice—when directed only to himself—but is more interested in mercy: that is to say, care for one's neighbors."[33] In "The Ethos of the Bible" we find the following: "All commands concerning outer (ritual) purity are robbed of their meaning. Not one syllable upholds any need of observing the ritual rules concerning purity which stand written in the law of Moses."[34]

Jesus' deeds form the background for his critical words, in which he defends his way of acting. When he goes to "lost" persons, "sinners," the "impure"—those who neither know the law nor follow it— he must then set himself above all prescriptions concerning purity which get in the way. The principle is that the basic commandment has priority and that other rules and regulations must give way so that it might be fulfilled.

This attitude of Jesus is permeated through and through with a totally unconventional judgment about people which is, at the same time, transcendent of all boundaries. He finds penitence and faith in publicans and adulterers, in a Gentile woman and in an officer in the heathen forces of occupation; he sets forth a child as an example of those who will come into the kingdom of God, and says that the immature understand more of his instruction than "the wise"; he turns no one away because he is a stranger, uncircumcised, or unaware of the rules concerning Sabbath and ritual conduct. Jesus breaks down the walls which have been built up around "the holy people" and lifts "the latent universalism in the ancient Hebrew faith" into the light by means of his central demand for a totally whole and open attitude toward God and man.

Jesus is "offensively generous" in his associations with people:

> It is extraordinarily peculiar that the Jesus who so radically sharpens God's demands can also demonstrate so radically how God forgives. He

44

is equally fastidious and demanding in his exposition of the Law as he is generous in respect to grace and forgiveness. . . . [The "lost ones"] suddenly get to experience something which they never could have dreamt: that they are highly regarded in the eyes of God *as they are,* deep in their cesspool, before they are able to rise up and wash themselves. . . . Without undertaking any investigation of a person's worthiness and without securing any guarantees about good relationships in the future, he can directly and unconditionally inform the person of the forgiveness of sins: "Be of good cheer my son, your sins are forgiven (by God)." Anyone who speaks in this way acts as though he has *authority.* He does something which a person according to the certainties of Judaism cannot do: he unconditionally gives the forgiveness of sins. He has unique consciousness of being the Son of God.

With such words Gerhardsson explains his thesis: "Jesus *is* already the gospel"—that is, already during the days of his earthly ministry.[35]

Looking back upon that which has been said concerning the ethical proclamation of Jesus we shall, finally, direct our attention to certain basic issues which Gerhardsson in part clearly accounts for and in part only glimpses. Matthew's interpretation of Jesus' attitude toward "the law" is built upon the fact that he radicalizes the generally-accepted juridical axiom that the basic law takes precedence over all other laws. It is the double commandment of love which plays the role of the basic law. That this double commandment is given priority by Jesus over all other laws is in and of itself incontestable. But when, in Matthew 5:18–19, in verses which in their form are "clearly technical-rabbinical," Matthew allows Jesus to say that not a dot of (the given) law shall pass away, such words "are not easily united" with the picture we otherwise get of Jesus' way of acting, with his sovereign ability to set aside laws and rules when the radical demand of love requires it. And furthermore, the demands which Jesus makes in interpreting any particular concrete commandment "demands an *inner attitude* which is infinitely more than the act of the commandment itself requires"—the demands have been brought "from the level of acting to 'the heart.'" This becomes less a question of law in the word's original meaning, of law as given rules, than of "a living, consistent, total attitude." The word "law" loses, in the ethical proclamation of Jesus, its actual content.

But Gerhardsson also provides other perspectives. In an article concerning Jesus' attitudes towards life, which has already been discussed, he speaks of a certain similarity between the argumentation of Jesus and the pedagogics of Socrates. This similarity lies in the desire to encounter the hearers' "consciences," to intensify what is already there. Gerhardsson refers to such appeals of Jesus as, "Why do you not judge for yourselves what is right?" (Luke 12:57). The difference is that Socrates here envisions "a natural disposition in man," while Jesus desires to make contact with "the capacities and insights which man *hitherto* has received, (from God)." But the difference, continues Gerhardsson, is not great: "Socrates thought religiously concerning the conscience of man, and Jesus saw no sharp distinction between that which man received from God at his birth and that which he received from him through proclamation, instruction, upbringing, and other influences within the community of the people of God."[36]

Somewhat further on in the same article Gerhardsson comes even closer to the same theme: in the vision of the final judgment, the only question which is raised is purely that of the works of mercy, or "love in practice." When Jesus reasons as he does, "he evidently presupposes that God has his general covenant with mankind, and mercy and responsible care are placed in hearts not only within the limits of the peculiar 'covenant' but also in a more general way. How Jesus regards this general relationship between the Creator and mankind is, however, not entirely easy to see."[37]

The Result

The intention of this overview of the research of Braun, Davies, and Gerhardsson has been to investigate how the problem of the earthly Jesus appears when one approaches it from different angles of vision: when, on the one hand, one attempts to look for that which was "non-Jewish" in him, and when, on the other hand, one finds it is important to clarify the continuity between Jesus and the heritage of Israel. The question now becomes whether the pictures of the earthly Jesus which have been drawn here are in unity or in conflict with one another. A comparison can, of course, only be made on the basis of the questions which have been dealt with by all three scholars. Since Braun is the only one of the three who has chosen to give a total picture of Jesus, it goes without saying that he has treated many questions which have not arisen in the work of the other two. That which can now be discussed is first and foremost the ethical proclamation of Jesus, a theme which each of the authors has dealt with extensively. Another important point of comparison concerns what can be described as the evangelical motif in Jesus' way of acting. All three authors speak to this, albeit in varying terminology: Braun uses the combination "radical demand—radical grace," Davies discusses "demand—grace," and Gerhardsson uses the term "radical demand—radical grace and unconditional forgiveness."

If we first view Jesus' ethical proclamation, our chief question becomes that of whether or not the different angles of approach lead to any actual differences among the scholars' descriptions of the content of this proclamation. The question can also be formulated: has the strong emphasis on the non-Jewish in Jesus led to an overemphasis on that which was unique in him? On the other hand, has interest in the continuity with the heritage of Israel led to a suppression of that which was unique in Jesus? The theme of Jesus and "the law" has been taken up in different ways by the three scholars: each has his own characteristic profile. But let us, to begin with, make clear that they all agree that we can arrive at a historically trustworthy picture of the content of Jesus' ethical teaching; likewise they agree as to the extraordinary importance this picture has for our knowledge of the earthly Jesus.

This strong accent on the importance of the ethical instruction of Jesus is in all three scholars fundamentally bound to a critical attitude toward that interpretation of Jesus which sees him only as an apocalyptic figure, a prophetic proclaimer that the "end-time" will soon arrive and subsequently be followed by the breaking in of the kingdom of God. This view, which ever since the days of Schweitzer has had great influence on Jesus research, is easily combined with the devaluation of the ethos of Jesus—which might thus have only an "interim" significance.

Not one of our trio of scholars contests the apocalyptic perspective in the gospels and in Jesus himself, but none will admit that this perspective should be determinative for Jesus' ethical instruction or that it should lead to a devaluation of that instruction. In this regard they are united, although their critical attitudes to the role played by the apocalyptic are formed in different ways.

By and large Braun has no objections—at any rate that are important—to the picture of Jesus as an apocalyptic figure as developed by the form-critical school in which he was nurtured. He declares, however, that Jesus was mistaken in sharing the apocalyptic ideas of his time. That was *ein Irrtum* which we must set aside. We can easily do this since the validity of this ethical proclamation is totally independent of these apocalyptic ideas. Davies does not see any connection between Jesus' frequent view of the imminent end of this age and "the clearsightedness" of his radical ethical proclamation—there can be no question of an "interim ethic." We have already seen that according to Gerhardsson the apocalyptic-eschatological perspective—in and of itself important—was strongly overemphasized in a large portion of the twentieth-century research concerning Jesus. It ought here to be observed that his critical position is motivated by his view that the source material does not warrant such an overemphasis. As will be indicated further on, the most recent research concerning Jesus confirms this view of the source material; it indicates that the apocalyptic elements in the gospels stem to a far higher degree from the tradition of the primitive church than from Jesus himself. It ought to be added, however, that the problem of Jesus and apocalypticism is extremely complex and that the attitude of current research toward this issue must be the object of closer examination in a later chapter.

Now to our principal consideration: there is no *substantive* difference between the views of these three scholars concerning the content of Jesus' ethical instruction. On the contrary, there is an obvious, not to say striking, agreement among them. The differences which do exist do not involve contradictions, at least in any fundamental sense, but are essentially complementary and can without difficulty be arranged in one total picture. That which is constitutive is the view that the proclamation of Jesus is thoroughly dominated by a *radical interpretation of the demand of love,* by the command to love God and to love one's neighbor, and that love of God and obedience to his will are realized in love and care for the neighbor.

This agreement first appears in that which is said concerning the relation between "love to God" and "love to the neighbor." None of the three have dealt as carefully and thoroughly with this theme as Gerhardsson. We remember how he started with the triple demand in the *Shema*—the central confession of Israel—and how he sought to show that the demand to love God with all one's heart, soul, and might resonates in the ethical proclamation of Jesus, even if the term "love to God" itself does not explicitly appear. At root everything which Jesus says concerning the proper relation to one's neighbor, and his entire radical interpretation of what is demanded, is a consequence of what

48

is involved in the proper relationship to God, which is obedience to his will. We do not find anything corresponding to this investigation in Braun, but this does not mean that Braun minimizes or reduces the relationship to God. For him also, the starting point of Jesus is "Jewish": one serves God by obeying him (*durch Gehorchen*)[38]—it is the content of this obedience that Jesus radicalizes. The word "love" itself seldom appears in the gospel texts, whether pertaining to God or the neighbor. The subject matter is there in overflowing measure; although it may seem that Jesus only speaks of one's relation to the neighbor, this is an illusion: God is present everywhere. The *Königsherrschaft* of God is a "central concept" in the proclamation of Jesus. "It is, in point of fact, always a question of God when Jesus speaks, even if love to God is not explicitly mentioned"; the proper relationship to the neighbor is at the same time the proper relationship to God, and vice versa.

If we examine what has been said about Jesus' radical interpretation of the love commandment and its consequences, it is immediately apparent that this radicalization has generally been given a double content. First, Jesus has sharpened the demand in a way which has no precedent, something which is clearly marked in that love is to include even enemies. The demand thus becomes universal and allows for no restrictions. Second, in Jesus it is not only a question of acts which are to be carried out, but also of the inner attitude toward life itself which is the basis for the act: this involves, for example, not only avoidance of acts of wrath but on the whole the refusal to nurse anger towards one's brother.

When Jesus sets forth the love commandment as the basic one, the commandment above all others, there are far-reaching consequences. None of the three scholars describe him as a revolutionary who attempted to overthrow the Jewish cult or the rules which prevailed at his time. However, all agree that every commandment, rule, and right must give way when they come into conflict with the love commandment: not only the contemporary interpretations of laws and rules, but also prescriptions in "the law of Moses" (for example, those concerning the Sabbath and purity). The commands which had ritual or observance character "are to be made light of," writes Gerhardsson— the corresponding expression in Braun is *Desinteresse* and *Vergleich- gültigung*.

All three scholars also agree that the radicalism in Jesus' ethical proclamation has been softened and modified in different ways by the tradition of the primitive church, which has set its stamp on the texts of the gospels. According to Davies, Matthew has shaped the "Sermon on the Mount" as the Torah of the Messiah, a Christian institution of law comparable to and competing with the contemporary attempt of the rabbis to make fast the tradition of Jewish law. Matthew has by a process of regulation softened the lack of compromise in the words of Jesus: "The need of the Church has dictated, if not created, much of the form and—probably—a part of the contents." From Gerhardsson we have learned that Matthew, this learned theologian schooled as a rabbi, in large measure left his personal imprint on the text of the gospel, and that his concern for preserving the connection with the spiritual heritage of Israel has caused him to modify the radicalism of Jesus.

Finally, all three scholars agree that Jesus, when he seeks to interpret how God desires life to be lived in conformity with the love commandment, does not support his words by reference to any authoritative title of honor. For example, he does not confirm his message by declaring that he speaks as the Messiah. When those who listen to him are convinced by him, this happens through the authoritative power of his words and person. The reaction is rendered trustworthy when it is indicated that he proclaimed with *exousia* ("power and authority") and not as the scribes. The evangelists, on the other hand, seek to defend the words and actions of Jesus by referring to some honorific title: both Matthew and Mark explain and defend the violation of the Sabbath by Jesus (and his disciples) by saying that "the Son of man is Lord over the Sabbath."

From what has now been said one cannot immediately conclude that Jesus had no interest in the question of messiahship. Jesus may in some sense have interpreted himself as the Messiah without allowing that messiahship to become a guarantee for the trustworthiness of his proclamation. This matter can be clarified by an argument which we find in Davies. He declares himself convinced that Jesus in reality desired to be the Messiah. But with not one word does he even hint that Jesus desired to authenticate his proclamation by reference to his messiahship. Davies stresses that the radical demand of Jesus is connected with his proclamation of the nearness of the kingdom of God, but there is no appeal to an outer, authoritative position of power in respect to either the demand or the proclamation. Jesus passed "beyond the light of Law and Prophet, to what we can only call an intuitive awareness of the will of God in its nakedness. . . . He himself in his intuitive awareness of the will of God is the source of the radical ethic."[39] Davies adds that the words of Jesus point beyond himself and become "witnesses to the King-Messiah." Such a statement must, however, become the subject of closer scrutiny. However this witness is to be viewed, it is obviously something totally other than the view that Jesus guaranteed the trustworthiness of his proclamation by claiming that he was and spoke as the Messiah.

The question of the relationship of Jesus to the titles of honor which are present in the gospels is a problem in itself—and an extremely complex one. We must at a later point examine how contemporary Jesus research views this matter. We are not able, for reasons of space, to extend our comparison among the three studies to include all of their details. But we have dealt with the main points, those which are of decisive importance, and our conclusion is that these different angles of vision by no means result in disparate pictures of Jesus' ethical proclamation. On the contrary, we have in all essentials a unified and clear picture of the wholeness and consistency of his teaching, a teaching which is borne by the radically-interpreted love commandment. It is still clear, to be sure, that the radicalism of Jesus has in different ways been modified in the texts of the gospels. Braun's approach has not obscured the continuity between Jesus and the heritage of Israel: he sheds ample light on the degree to which Jesus finds himself on the Judaic plane. When, on the other hand, Gerhardsson presents a far deeper analysis of the theme "I have come not to abolish . . . but to fulfill," this does not restrict the radical character of his words or the sovereignty of his way of acting—the fulfillment consists precisely in the radicalization of the twofold love command.

It is in this context highly important to note that the term "the law," according to all three scholars, basically loses the meaning which the word has traditionally possessed. What Jesus gives us is not an interpretation of the law in the manner of the rabbis, but, to quote Davies, his "intuitive awareness of the will of God in its nakedness." The demands which he sets forth are not only for an outward, literal pursuit of fixed commands, but for an attitude towards life determined by love: "a living, consistent and total attitude" (Gerhardsson). And so, when this section of the Sermon on the Mount concludes with the words "You, therefore, must be perfect, as your heavenly Father is perfect," it is obviously no longer possible to speak of law in the original meaning of the words. "Perfect"—in Greek, *teleios*—means, writes Gerhardsson, "whole, undivided, unharmed, irreproachable in the attitude of one's heart and thus in all of one's actions towards God and man."

This picture of the ethical proclamation of Jesus surely poses many questions. To some of these we shall return later. But *one* question must be dealt with now. How does Jesus' radical demand relate to that which we can know in general about his proclamation and about his association with people? As has already been pointed out, we find in all three scholars a juxtaposition of "radical demand and radical grace"—the term itself, as Braun has indicated, scarcely appears in the Synoptic Gospels, but it is expressed abundantly through a number of other terms. All three are agreed that in Jesus the radical demand is bound to radical "grace." He goes directly to the "lost"; he bestows on man—unconditionally—the forgiveness of sins. It is worthy of notice and consideration that Braun and Gerhardsson, when they deal with this theme, express themselves in remarkably similar ways. Braun writes: "It is a well-known phenomenon in the history of religions that, when serious and uncompromising demands are placed, such rigorism usually leads to a discrimination between humans which represent another point of view." The "surprising" and "perplexing" thing is that Jesus acts in the very opposite way.[40] Gerhardsson writes: "It is highly peculiar that the Jesus who sharpens the demands of God can demonstrate so radically how God forgives." Braun asserts his view concerning Jesus' way of acting in the surprising thesis (surprising especially if one thinks of the theological school to which he belongs) that Jesus himself belongs to the gospel which he proclaims. He does this by referring not to messiahship or to honorific titles, but by referring to his actual manner of dealing with people. Gerhardsson accentuates Braun's formula: when Jesus acts as he does "he *is* already the gospel." According to Gerhardsson, Jesus does not rest his claim on any title, but his actions bear witness to his unique consciousness concerning that which is the will of God.

The theme which has been reviewed above is certainly a principal theme in Jesus research. What has been said at the conclusion of our comparison between Braun, Davies, and Gerhardsson functions as a bridge to our next chapter, where the theme in question will be scrutinized in greater detail with reference to broader studies concerning Jesus.

Notes

1. W. D. Davies, *The Sermon on the Mount* (Cambridge: Cambridge University Press, 1966). Cf. also W. D. Davies, *The Setting of the Sermon on the Mount* (Cambridge: Cambridge University Press, 1966).

2. Birger Gerhardsson, "Bibelns ethos," *Etik och kristen tro*, ed. Gustaf Wingren (Lund: Gleerups, 1971), pp. 13–92. Also published in offprint form.

3. Herbert Braun, *Jesus* (Stuttgart: Kreuz, 1969), p. 52.

4. Ibid., p. 61.

5. Ibid., p. 87.

6. Ibid., p. 145.

7. Ibid., pp. 157–58.

8. Ibid., pp. 159ff.

9. Ibid., p. 167.

10. Ibid., p. 170.

11. Birger Gerhardsson in the collection *Ur Nya testamentet* (Lund: Gleerups, 1970), p. 113.

12. Davies, *The Sermon on the Mount*, p. 6.

13. Ibid., p. 4.

14. Ibid., p. 85.

15. Ibid., p. 90.

16. Ibid., pp. 15–16.

17. Ibid., p. 23.

18. Ibid., p. 28.

19. Ibid., p. 109.

20. Ibid., p. 114.

21. Ibid., p. 126.

22. Ibid., p. 134.

23. Ibid., p. 142.

24. Ibid., pp. 143–44.

25. Ibid., p. 147.

26. Ibid., p. 148.

27. Ibid., p. 150.

28. Ibid., p. 155.

29. Birger Gerhardsson, *The Testing of God's Son,* trans. John Toy (Lund: Gleerups, 1966); *Ur Nya testamentet* (Lund: Gleerups, 1970); "Bibelns ethos," pp. 13–92; and *2000 år senare* (Stockholm: Verbum, 1972).

30. Birger Gerhardsson, "Geistiger Opferdienst nach Matth. 6, 1–6,, 16–21," *Neues Testament und Geschichte. Historisches Geschehen und Deutung im Neuen Testament. Oscar Cullmann zum 70. Geburtstag,* ed. Heinrich Baltensweiler and Bo Reicke (Zürich/Tübingen: Theologischer Verlag / J. C. B. Mohr [Paul Siebeck], 1972).

31. Birger Gerhardsson, "The Parable of the Sower and Its Interpretation," *New Testament Studies,* vol. 14, 1967–68; "The Seven Parables in Matthew XIII," *New Testament Studies,* vol. 19, 1972–73; also in "Du Judéo-Christianisme à Jésus par le Shema'," *Recherches de Science Réligieuse,* 1972.

32. Gerhardsson, "Bibelns ethos," p. 43.

33. Gerhardsson, *2000 år senare,* p. 77.

34. Gerhardsson, "Bibelns ethos," p. 40.

35. Gerhardsson, *2000 år senare,* pp. 128ff.

36. Ibid., p. 69–70.

37. Ibid., p. 80.

38. Braun, *Jesus,* p. 60.

39. Davies, *The Sermon on the Mount,* pp. 148–49.

40. Braun, *Jesus,* pp. 66–67.

41. Gerhardsson, *2000 år senare,* pp. 128ff.

3

THE CHALLENGER

Accusations against Jesus

That the leaders among Jesus' contemporaries found him "challenging" is something we have already discovered. This important theme, however, demands closer investigation, and we shall undertake our examination in the light of recent Jesus research.

The cause for the irritation present among the Jews of Jesus' time does not seem to have been his teaching. Primarily at issue was his behavior, his way of acting. Four categories of acts were attacked: (1) acts which involved violation of the law—not only of the contemporary interpretation of the law, but also of "the law of Moses"; (2) the driving out of evil spirits by Beelzebul; (3) his association and table fellowship with ostracized people, "sinners and publicans"; and (4) his blasphemy in claiming to bestow the forgiveness of sins, something reserved to God alone.

The first of these accusations we have already dealt with in sufficient detail. We shall therefore begin with the second: exorcism, or the driving out of "evil spirits." The conflict concerned neither the existence of evil spirits nor whether there was such a thing as the driving out of demons—there was no doubt at these points. The controversial issue was how these exorcisms were to be interpreted.

In Jesus' time it belonged to the order of the day to speak of evil, demonic spirits and their devastating influence on man. It was also assumed that satanically-inspired "prophets" were able by their miracles to seduce the people. Such were the presuppositions for the attack on Jesus: his healing of the ill by "driving out evil spirits" was a diabolic delusion—he was satanically inspired and a false prophet. The gospels speak of different reactions on the part of Jesus. Even though one or the other of the gospels may ultimately have been influenced by later situations in the primitive church, there need be no doubt concerning the why and how of Jesus' reactions. He pointed out, among other things, that the charges of his accusors were absurd: a satanic power could not act as he had been charged to do without liquidating itself. The driving out of evil spirits put Jesus in a diametrically opposed context: the coming kingdom of God.

C. H. Dodd has dealt extensively with the issue of exorcism. He takes a word from Jesus from Luke, generally considered authentic, as a point of departure: "If by the finger of God I drive out the devils, then be sure the kingdom of God has come upon you" (11:20). Dodd writes: "The saying is obviously figurative. To speak literally, God has no fingers, and there may not be such things as evil spirits; what the Gospels call casting out devils we might describe, rightly or wrongly, in other terms. But the essential meaning is not obscure. In the presence of Jesus, the dark forces within, which ravage the souls and bodies of men, were overcome and their victims made new." There is no reason, continues Dodd, to doubt that this was the way Jesus acted. For Jesus, exorcism was a sign of the coming kingdom of God: not that "Jesus brought in, or set up, the kingdom of God," but that God, active in his creation and standing behind everything, had brought about this "significant moment."[1]

Another contemporary work on Jesus is Norman Perrin's *Rediscovering the Teaching of Jesus* (1956). He points out that the peculiar expression God's "finger" can be found in Exodus 8:19. Jesus used this term from the Old Testament in his interpretation of the exorcisms; they were not worked by demons, but by God. Such being the case, men here and now can experience "the new Exodus"; the exorcisms are, in other words, a manifestation of the functioning of God's kingdom. The sect of Qumran shaped its eschatological expectations in terms of a holy war between "the Sons of Light and the Sons of Darkness." This motif of conflict is also central for Jesus: the battle is between good and evil, between God and Satan. When exorcism is viewed from this perspective it testifies not only to God's victory in general; the important thing is that this power manifests itself here and now, experienced by restored and renewed individuals. To Perrin, concentration on the individual and his experience is a striking feature of the teaching of Jesus, and in this lies an all-important difference from Qumran.[2]

It is clear that according to both Dodd and Perrin such "miracles" are to be seen in relation to Jesus' central message of the coming kingdom of God—indeed, such seems to have been Jesus' own interpretation. This view is of course not invalidated if one stresses that Jesus addressed himself to individuals; the totality is revealed in individual cases. We find the same interpretation of the exorcisms in Amos N. Wilder's *The Language of the Kingdom* (1964). If, writes Wilder, one is to understand correctly the meaning of the accounts of how Jesus drove out evil spirits—anecdotes, stories, narratives—as preserved by the primitive church, they must be read in relation to what is said about Jesus' activity in its entirety. The intention of this activity "had to do not just with the driving out of demons from the few but with dispossession of Satan generally." Wilder is convinced both that many of these healings have historical backgrounds and that they are not to be regarded as isolated incidents. They are characteristic traits in the "world-changing drama in which he was the principal." Incidents of this kind were intended to demonstrate "the finger of God in the land of the living" and were typical episodes in Jesus' all-inclusive work of liberation. The accounts in question "carry the whole Gospel in a nutshell—victories over Satan, the demolishing of obstacles, including hard hearts, and the incursions of love."[3]

In this context a few words about the miracles of Jesus can be parenthetically added. The exorcisms constitute one part in a series of healing miracles. Braun's statement that he cannot in rationalistic cocksureness contest all that is reported concerning the miracles of Jesus, and especially not his miracles of healing, may be taken as representative of the position of many scholars. There is frequent emphasis on how characteristic it was for Jesus not only to be concerned with "the spiritual" but also with the bodily welfare of people; Jesus' healings are an important part of his whole activity. In Jesus' time there was nothing unusual about narratives about the working of miracles. The unique thing about the "mighty acts" of Jesus was that they were set in connection with and interpreted as a sign of the coming kingdom of God. Recent research has often pointed out that the miracles have a typological precedent in the Old Testament—thus, for example, the manna given to Israel in the desert is a "type" of Jesus' miracles of feeding. In other cases the miracles attributed to Jesus correspond to the eschatological expectations of late Judaism concerning the messianic age. A form-critical investigation of how the accounts developed in the different gospels shows that the miracles may have originated and been enlarged upon in the course of tradition. It may also be that what was originally a parable may have been transformed into an event. This seems to be the case with what was said about the fig tree—in Luke it is a parable (13:6–9); Mark and Matthew describe it as the miracle of the withering fig tree (Mark 11:12–14, 20–21; Matt. 21:20–21). It would be more than simple boldness to think that anyone can determine the facts behind all of the different miracle stories.

We can now return to the accusations made against Jesus. The charge, basically without rhyme or reason, that he drove out evil spirits by the power of Beelzebul, would hardly have been made without something more basic in mind. The driving out of evil spirits, to use the expression of the time, was in and of itself no cause for criticism. When, nonetheless, this activity of Jesus was described as demonically inspired, the charge must have been based on the fact that his actions and patterns of behavior were interpreted from another angle. This "other angle" leads directly to the next accusation, that Jesus associated with "sinners and publicans."

The controversy concerning Jesus' style of association with the people had a totally different character than the previous one. Now his opponents really meant business, and it is not difficult to understand why. The accusation that Jesus drove out evil spirits by the power of Beelzebul had no factual basis; the criticism of his associations with people was quite different. Here was something to hang on to; here one could refer to acts of Jesus which *must* have been so highly offensive in the eyes of his contemporaries that they doubtlessly contributed to the growing animosity which finally led to the crucifixion.

The gospels devote considerable attention to describing these conflicts, and there is considerable agreement that we are dealing here with historically trustworthy material. That, however, does not mean that the events must have taken place exactly as the texts indicate. Yet even if the accounts have been stylized, they have nonetheless a paradigmatic trustworthiness, an incontestable inner truth; they give us a faithful picture of Jesus and the people to whom he was devoted. If we think of another side of the conflict, of the sharp words which Jesus directed towards "the scribes and the pharisees," it becomes by no means certain that the gospels have reported exactly what Jesus said. It is probable that several of the most critical sayings originated

58

in the tradition, in situations which, at least as far as Matthew is concerned, were determined by the sharp opposition between the young church and contemporary rabbinic Judaism. But even if not everything written about Jesus is authentic, it does not follow that we have to be doubtful about how he reacted toward his critics and slanderers; his attitude is clearly made manifest not only in direct, sharp, and revealing words, but also in a series of parables preserved by the gospels. To be sure, the gospels include parables which developed in order to apply to given situations in the life of the early church, but these are rather easily discernible and do not hide the identity of the parables' original addressees or what Jesus had to say to them.

When, time and again, the gospels speak of how freely, naturally, and with friendship Jesus associated with "publicans and sinners," we must not get the impression that Jesus only had contact with people who were despised in contemporary Judaism. He undoubtedly associated with all kinds of people: with "common folk," with representatives of the different elements within contemporary Judaism, and at times also with strangers. Those who went by the name of publicans and sinners were but a small minority among those who listened to him and followed him, but his association with just this minority aroused enormous attention and became a real scandal in the community.

"Publicans and sinners" is a common combination in the gospels. Both were ostracized—the sinners on religious grounds, the publicans on both religious and social grounds. Sinners were those who had ignored and violated the law and its regulations. The occupation of the publicans was to collect taxes for the Roman occupation forces, and by performing this despised task it was held that they had made heathens of themselves—in other words, they had set themselves outside the Jewish community. When scholars today wish to describe them in contemporary terminology, they can speak of the publicans as "Quislings." The word meets us in different combinations: Matthew speaks of being "as a Gentile and a tax collector" (18:17); the pharisee in the temple places the publican in the company of "extortioners, unjust, adulterers" (Luke 18:11). The publicans had a well-known reputation for cheating on the job; in the Jewish literature of that time they are often spoken of in the same context as thieves. The situation of the publicans led to a degree of isolation which reminds us of the extreme apartheid in South Africa today. Religiously, they were conceived of as contagious; if a publican entered the home of a law-abiding Jew, the house could thereby become "unclean."[4] It is against this background that one must understand Jesus' admonition to the "chief priests and the elders" in Jerusalem: ". . . the tax collectors and the harlots go into the kingdom of God before you" (Matt. 21:31).

The offense caused by Jesus' habits of association was heightened by the fact that he ate with those who had been ostracized. He was able to invite them to the meals which he shared, during his wanderings, with his disciples; on occasion he was also a guest in the home of publicans. To share table-fellowship with such people was, in the eyes of the Jews, a thing of no insignificance—it was a sign of extreme intimacy and closeness. They were deeply shocked pharisees who asked, when Jesus visited the home of Levi the publican, "Why does he eat with tax collectors and sinners?" (Mark 2:16). Table fellowship with "sinners" was not a simple breach of etiquette on the part of the individual, it was a clear defiance of both the regulations concerning purity and the ordinances which prescribed the penance required of such violators of the law for restoration into the religious and social community.

The reaction to Jesus' sharing of meals with publicans and sinners is thus fully explainable. And yet it must be stated that there was a stronger reason for this reaction, insofar as those who were shocked well understood the actual intention of Jesus. This problem appears in the gospels in connection with the question of why the disciples of Jesus, in contrast to those of John the Baptist, did not fast (Mark 2:18–22; Matt. 9:14–17; Luke 5:33–39). This theme is treated in many ways by contemporary scholars (who on the whole are most interested in the texts concerning common meals), and especially thoroughly by Jürgen Roloff.[5]

Jesus' answer to the question of why his disciples did not fast is, according to Mark: *"Can the wedding guests fast while the bridegroom is with them?* As long as they have the bridegroom with them, they cannot fast. The days will come, when the bridegroom is taken away from them, and then they will fast in that day" (2:10–20). It is generally held that the words which we have italicized are authentic, and that the words not italicized stem from the tradition of the early church. Roloff holds to this position and partially explains his conclusion by pointing out that the word "bridegroom" as Jesus' self-designation has a hidden content, taking on a messianic connotation in the latter part of the verse. In addition, there is a shift in the perspective: in the authentic words (v. 19) the emphasis is on the present, with only a weak intimation of a coming separation; in the latter words (v. 20) that separation is emphasized.

The meaning of Jesus' words is not to proclaim any abolition of fasting—there is, says Roloff, no reason to doubt the authenticity of the instructions given by Jesus on another occasion concerning a "right" fast, which is distinguished from a fast designed to be "seen by men" (Matt. 6:16–18).[6] "The fasting of the disciples of John may have been justified—for the disciples of Jesus it would have been a misunderstanding of the present time if they had devoted themselves to asceticism; for *now* it is more important to participate in table fellowship with the bridegroom than it is to fast."[7] The question of the different attitudes towards fasting held by the disciples of John and Jesus has been answered: precisely because of Jesus his disciples lived in a new and totally different situation.

If the critics of Jesus did not grasp the full significance of the threat involved in this table fellowship, they fully understood the threat which lay in the fact that Jesus offered the forgiveness of sins to people. The account of this offer is held by scholars to be quite totally authentic. In the description given in Mark 2:5–10, writes Braun, the offer of the forgiveness of sins is a typical feature of Jesus' activity: "It must be historically correct that Jesus bestowed on such people in their concrete situation 'on earth' the forgiveness of sins."[8] The critics of Jesus were immediately ready with their judgment: "It is blasphemy! Who can forgive sins but God alone?" (Mark 2:7). They had no alternative but to regard such deeds and words as the height of all threats. From their point of view they were correct—it cannot be refuted that Jesus here acts on behalf of God as a representative of the kingdom of God.

Self-Defense and Attack

Jesus reacted to the criticism of the "scribes and pharisees" by self-defense and attack. The attack was sometimes indirectly hidden in self-defense; sometimes it was direct. In his encounters Jesus used not only direct criticism, but also—and with great effectiveness—parables and example stories: the lost sheep, the lost coin, the prodigal son; the pharisee and the publican in the temple.

Contemporary scholarship has endeavored to present a nuanced picture of Jesus' controversy with the pharisees. When some pharisees, as we have previously observed, emphasized the priority of the double commandment of love, they were undeniably in affinity with Jesus' own interpretation of the law: the scribe who speaks in this spirit is told by Jesus that he is "not far from the kingdom of God" (Mark 12:34). In judging the encounter of Jesus with the pharisees one must also consider the fact that the gospels were formed and edited during a time of increasing conflict between the young church in Palestine and the Judaism which was struggling to stabilize and solidify its position through an ever more rigorous interpretation of the law. There can be no doubt that this conflict played a role in the formation of the criticism directed by the gospels against the pharisees.

One of Jesus' sharpest criticisms of the pharisees concerned their "hypocrisy"; they "do all their deeds to be seen by men." Jesus undoubtedly encountered people of this sort, and he revealed the wrong side of their piety with a sharpness which etches itself in the mind and lastingly stamps such a pattern of behavior as dreadful and frightening. But two things ought to be remembered in this connection: first, Jesus' attack concerned individual pharisees and not Pharisaism as a whole; and secondly, such a critique was also expressed by the pharisees themselves.

Jesus also accuses the pharisees of "preaching but not doing": "The scribes and the Pharisees sit on Moses' seat; so practice and observe whatever they tell you, but not what they do; for they preach, but do not practice" (Matt. 23:2). There are strong indications that this polemical chapter has been severely stylized, as probably have also been these particular words. Jesus may well have given his approval to "the watch of the scribes and pharisees" over the law of Moses— but the formula "practice and observe whatever they tell you" has without doubt a specific Matthaean color. Concerning the accusation "they preach, but do not practice," one must also bear in mind that Jesus directed a similar charge against his own: it does not help to *say* if one does not *do* the will of the heavenly Father—such a person is like a foolish man who builds his house upon the sand (Matt. 7:21–27).

If such considerations lend much-needed nuance to the picture of Jesus' relation to the pharisees, the sharpness of the controversy is nonetheless not lessened—it was in reality sharper and more basic than any of the other conflicts described in the gospels. When all is said and done, this more nuanced picture clarifies what was actually decisive in the conflict between Jesus and the pharisees. Is it surprising that the conflict became the hottest in a case in which there existed a certain affinity? Hardly—for precisely then did it become necessary for Jesus to let his message be heard in all its radicality. Pharisaism was a reform movement—Jesus placed new wine in new skins (Matt. 9:19, Mark 2:22).

In order to investigate this matter more closely, we shall turn to a few of the parables which were obviously intended in self-defense. The amount of literature concerning Jesus' parables is extraordinarily large; the most celebrated twentieth-century studies are C. H. Dodd's *The Parables of the Kingdom,* Joachim Jeremias's *The Parables of Jesus,* Amos Wilder's previously mentioned *The Language of the Gospel,* Eta Linnemann's *Jesus of the Parables,* and Dan O. Via's *The Parables: Their Literary and Existential Dimension.*[9]

Eta Linnemann presents in her book an accomplished and clear interpretation of the parables which, to judge from its several editions, has been appreciated by a wide reading public. The interpretation is form-critically oriented, but at the same time the book pursues the German tradition of parable research most notably presented in the work of Jeremias. Among its characteristic features are the theses that the parables aim at presenting only one central theme (the "one point interpretation") and that they must be understood in their "historical setting" as they must have been understood by the original listeners. It is generally accepted by scholarship that the parables of the gospels have in fact been placed within the context of the primitive church, and that it is therefore necessary to go behind the gospels in order to arrive at their original meaning.

A strong tendency within recent parable interpretation is to make them the object of linguistic and semantic analysis. Wilder's book on "early Christian rhetoric" has such an intention. His investigation is of wide scope. In the section which deals with the parables, Wilder describes them as "stories" taken from "secular" life. These momentary pictures have an enormous impact: they reveal how the destiny of people is decided as they take positions in actual situations. When Jesus clothes his message in the form of parables and uses them for the purposes of self-defense or attack, he does so in order to make or even force those who listen to take a consciously responsible position. In this context Wilder registers a certain reservation against the train of thought set forth by Harald Riesenfeld.[10] As do all recent scholars, Riesenfeld dismisses earlier allegorical interpretations. For him the parables have quite definite meanings and intentions; they are always, in different ways, expressions of the central message of Jesus. But they may, simultaneously, have a certain secondary allegorical meaning in their use of the Old Testament terms such as shepherd, king, vineyard, etc. Such well-known expressions immediately arouse definite associations for the listeners. For example, to speak of a shepherd causes one to think of the Psalm which begins, "The Lord is my shepherd." Wilder does not wish to deny that certain parables can call forth such associations: "We should not be so rigid as to exclude all such overtones. But the impact of the parables lay in their immediate realistic authenticity. In the parable of the Lost Sheep the shepherd is an actual shepherd and not a flash-back to God as the Shepherd of Israel or to the hoped-for Messiah who will shepherd Israel."

This discussion is of special interest since it is basically a confrontation between two contemporary tendencies. When Riesenfeld speaks of associations with the Old Testament, this is typical of a trend in research which is concerned with clarifying the relationship between the parables of Jesus and similar material—*ha mashal*—in the Old Testament and in later Jewish literature. No direct contradiction need arise between this trend and the one represented by Wilder. It is rather a question of emphases which can complement each other. And in *one* respect they undoubtedly have a common interest to safeguard: neither is content with the "one point interpretation" which for so long has played a prominent role in the interpretation of the parables. This will become more apparent as we turn to the most original of these recent works on the parables—Dan Via's *The Parables*.

A chief point for Via is that the parables must primarily be seen as whole entities, as artistic literary creations. They have their own autonomy and must be understood in their own "cohesive unity," not to be divided into form and content. This would be to reduce form to only a protective cover for the content, and thus to misunderstand the significance which form itself has. From this point of departure, Via criticizes the "one point" theory of interpretation as a method which breaks the unity of the parable, draws attention away from the parable as a total entity, and thus reduces its ability to function as "a language event." By frequently using this expression, Via desires to say that the parable not only reports an event, it functions itself as an event. It accomplishes something; it "declares war or opens a highway." The parable is a language event because it injects a new possibility into the situation of the listeners and because it demands that they take a personal position. Via also criticizes the method of interpreting a parable which first locates the situation of its origin; basically "it is not ultimately the text which is interpreted and clarified, but the interpreter and his situation are illuminated." Via, therefore, desires to interpret the message and work of Jesus in the light of his parables and—secondarily—the parables in the light of his "ministry." One result of Via's view is that the relationship between Jesus and his parables is seen as two-sided and, to a certain degree, paradoxical. The parables are in a totally unique way determined by Jesus and his power of illustration; in these artistic creations he himself is encountered far more immediately than in his other statements. But at the same time these literary, aesthetic entities possess a "relative autonomy" and live their own lives, so to speak, through the inherent power of language. In summary, Via asserts that the parables are especially designed to express the new existential situation brought about by Jesus, and that they therefore function as a language event.[11]

Yet another work devoted to linguistic analysis must be mentioned in this context: Robert W. Funk's *Language, Hermeneutic, and Word of God: The Problem of Language in the New Testament and Contemporary Theology.*[12] In the section dealing with the parables, Funk stresses—as does Via— their extraordinary importance. It is not simply that the parables have a message to bring; they *are* in themselves the message which Jesus brings: admonishing, challenging, and at the same time inviting. They cannot without impairment be verbalized into nonparabolic language. In the parables Jesus allows a new world to take shape, a world constituted by "the new logic of grace."

Many of Jesus' parables lay bare the decisive opposition between himself and the pharisees. This is true not least with the parables which deal with the "lost"—the lost sheep, the lost coin, the prodigal son.

Two versions of the parable of the lost sheep appear (Matt. 18:12–13 and Luke 15:1–7). Matthew has placed this parable in a context which deals with church order in the primitive Christian community. The two verses which frame the parable clearly show that Matthew intended the parable to serve as an admonition to the Christian congregation not to "despise one of these little ones." In this context the basic meaning of the parable has been obscured and the situation in which it was formed is lost from sight. In Luke, on the contrary, it is completely clear that the parable has to do with the conflict between Jesus and the pharisees and that its background is the storm which Jesus aroused by his contact with "tax collectors and sinners." The accent placed by the parable upon recovery and the joy of recovery shows that of primary importance is not human penance but rather the "act of grace"; salvation and penance, so to speak, exchange places. This turned upside down the pharisees' conception of the proper relationship between penance and liberation. They certainly held that according to God's law sinners could be restored to the community, but their position unavoidably presupposed that sinners must give clear proof of penance—and one could not find a sign of such penance among the sinners with whom Jesus associated.

As we now turn to the parable of the prodigal son we must observe the positions of the different interpreters, paying attention also to an author whose work we have not this far noted: K. H. Rengstorf's *Die Re-Investitur des Verlorenen Sohnes in der Gleichniserzählung Jesu Luk 15:11–32.*[13] There is general agreement that the background of this parable is the "rumbling" among the scribes and pharisees over Jesus' association with publicans and sinners, and that the parable provides Jesus' answer to their complaints. Scholars also agree that the parable is not an allegory: the father is not God, and the elder brother does not stand for the pharisees. But at the same time, the interpretations indicate rich and varying associations in the story. The picture of the younger son recalls "the sinners" with whom Jesus associated, and his behavior in the foreign land alludes to the publicans. The feast at the return of the son is reminiscent of Jesus' table-fellowship with those who were "unworthy." The picture of the father harks back to Old Testament words concerning how God can act; the picture of the elder brother alludes to the pharisees. The points of the parable which demand special attention chiefly involve the protagonists, the father and the two brothers, but also, on the other hand, the way in which those who listened to the parable reacted.

Our first question, then, is: what constituted the sin of the younger brother? There is no doubt that his behavior in the foreign land was "sinful" in two respects: he irresponsibly squandered his inheritance, and he hired himself out as a swineherd in the service of a foreigner. This latter act was an obvious violation of the law by which he acted as a renegade and a "heathen"—and here we recall the image of the publicans as pawns of the Roman occupation forces. Yet it is another question whether or not the parable blames the younger son for having left his father's home. Via is of the opinion that the parable was conceived in these terms and that the listeners were also inclined to judge it in this way.[14] Linnemann adopts a different position. At the time of Jesus it was common that young Jews sought their fortunes by emigrating to a foreign land—more Jews lived abroad than in Palestine. No legal objection could be raised against the son receiving his share of the inheritance with the right to use it, nor could the listeners understand the wish of the son as an "impertinent demand."[15] Rengstorf, on the other hand, sharpens the judgment: the younger son has by his behavior cut all ties with his family.[16]

The next question concerns the decision of the famished son to return home. He is aware that he has sinned against God and his father, but in spite of everything he entertains the hope of being able to serve as a slave in his old home. That in his desperate situation he tries to save his life by returning home seems quite natural. Via stresses that his train of thought is totally oriented to the law and thus to the punishment which is demanded. He has lost his sonship and is deserving of only rejection. But he still dares count with the possibility that by grace the punishment might be mild enough to allow him to stay at home as one of the hired servants.

We come to the picture of the father. Dodd writes that here "is no ideal picture of an imaginary father, of such exceptional saintliness that he can stand for God himself. He is *any* father worth the name, as the hearers are expected to recognize . . ."[17] Perrin has less confidence in the understanding of the listeners: many, and especially those to whom the story was addressed, must have conceived of the returning son as dead in the eyes of any self-respecting Jewish father. The father's entire disposition towards his son is described in the parable as "extravagant," a highly intentional disposition which is encountered in every detail of the parable—even down to the father's running to meet the son.[18] In connection with this maneuver of the father, Jeremias has reflected that it was most unusual and unworthy for an aged Oriental to come running in such a fashion—a reflection which has been repeated by Perrin as well as Linnemann and Via.

The reception given by the father to the returning son was, according to Linnemann, by no means an everyday event. The embrace and the kiss attest to the fact that the lost son had been forgiven and reinstated in his sonship, and that this happened even before he could confess his guilt. Every element in the following description—up to the feast and the dance—bears witness to the rehabilitation of the son and to the father's overwhelming joy. The listeners must have had difficulty in viewing the father's behavior as something self-evident; but on the other hand the story need not have been interpreted as totally unreasonable and impossible. To speak of a father's mercy was to call to mind a familiar picture of God's mercy (cf. Psalm 103:13). It could not have escaped the listeners that Jesus' story alluded to his own way of associating with sinners—what he describes is how a sinner "turns around," forced to act by the squalor of his existence, and how he is then received with overwhelming mercy. No proof that he has actually changed is demanded. Does the event of the parable really involve such a conversion? When Jesus told his story he was more than aware of the strict demand for penance on the part of the listeners. Could he then expect his hearers to see things in the same way as he did? The extraordinary power of this parable made it difficult for the listeners to be totally unmoved.

The father's generous welcome of the returning son depends, writes Via, not on any set conditions or proof of repentance.[19] "In fact repentance finally turns out to be the capacity to forego pride and accept graciousness."

The father's way of acting was surprising but not unthinkable. He took risks—of being regarded as compliant, of encouraging his son in his degradation, of wronging the elder brother—but he took those risks.

68

In deciding to return home, the son's thoughts had revolved around the demands of the law. When he was subsequently welcomed by his father, he found himself in a situation which was qualitatively different from anything he might have imagined. The insight which the parable wishes to bring to the fore is that "natural man's legalistic understanding of the divine-human relationship is shattered only by the unexpected degree of forgiveness which comes to him from beyond himself."[20]

Rengstorf's book concerning the prodigal son's "re-investiture" exemplifies that trend in current scholarship which seeks to clarify the relationship between the parables of Jesus and the Jewish heritage. His investigation is concentrated around the father's words to his servants: "Bring quickly the best robe, and put it on him; and put a ring on his hand, and shoes on his feet" (Luke 15:22). This element in the story has a legal, juridical character, directly related to contemporary Jewish usage. It involves re-investiture, a rehabilitation, and a restoration of the lost son's status as a son. The younger son had doubtless been counseled against leaving the family. When he nevertheless did that, he was cut off from the family, reckoned as non-existant—"dead," as the father said. The "best robe" was the formal dress which he had once worn as a son and left behind when he travelled away, and which he now received again. The ring was, as throughout the Orient, a symbol of power. The shoes were a sign not only of a status other than that of the servants, but also—as Rengstorf indicates by Old Testament references—of a lordly position, albeit subordinate to the father. Rengstorf finds that there is something of the Oriental court running through this entire story. The re-investiture means that the lost son, the sinner, has now rightly and without restrictions been reinstated as "the hereditary son." That which takes place is a *justificatio impii*—a justification of the ungodly.[21]

Finally, a few comments concerning the picture of the elder son, the heavily weighted conclusion of the parable. When the elder brother says, "Lo, these many years I have served you, and I never disobeyed your command," Dodd discerns a satirical criticism of the pharisees. Linnemann also holds that these words refer to the pharisees, but this does not mean that the elder brother must reflect them in other respects. His protest is different than the one which they directed towards Jesus: namely, "How can you eat with such people?" The elder son does not complain over the father's behavior toward him, nor over the fact that he has been denied the service of the slaves (as has sometimes been held), nor over the fact that he has been held on too short reins by his father. That which he protests is the enormity of the feast for the returning brother: there was not sufficient reason for such a grandiose reception. The father seeks to convince him to the contrary. This case was totally extraordinary—"This your brother was dead, and he is alive"—therefore there is good reason for the elder brother himself to share the joy. According to Perrin, the elder son has been correctly described in accordance with the current Jewish understanding of the demands of law and justice. The parable does not describe him as a malevolent person. His attitude is, if one honestly considers the legalistic presuppositions from which he reasons, consistent and irreproachable. Via, for his part, claims that there is a shadow over the elder son. He misunderstands his relation to his father; his thoughts revolve around the question of merit and reward, and this prevents a deep personal relationship between son and father.

It is apparent that there are differences between scholars' views of the behavior of the elder son. That the parable is critical of the elder son cannot be denied, but at the same time it is not evident that the parable portrays him as a villain. If we ask what the parable—indirectly—has to say about the relation of Jesus to the pharisees, it is apparent, as Dodd says, that there is a somewhat satirical edge against them presented in the figure of the elder son. But neither here nor in what the parable says as a whole is there a desire to abuse or revile the pharisees. The parable intended to clarify the actual grounds for the opposition between Jesus and the pharisees, and it has accomplished this with extraordinary precision.

Further light can be shed on Jesus' relation to the pharisees in the account of the pharisee and the publican in the temple (Luke 18:9–14). Christian proclamation has traditionally regarded the pharisee of this text as the prototype for hypocritical and arrogant piety and the publican as the humble sinner. Jesus' listeners could not possibly have interpreted the story that way. The pharisee described by Jesus is an ideal example of a pious person; there is no mention of any hypocrisy. With forthright joy the pharisee thanks God that he has been able to fast more and give more than the required tithe. The phrase "I thank thee that I am not like other men . . ." is not an expression of hypocritical presumptuousness but rather of genuine gratitude: for all that he had been able to do he gives—so it seems—the honor to God, and he regards it all as a gift from God, a proof of God's grace toward him. Those who heard Jesus must certainly have understood this pharisee as a man of God. The publican, in contrast, was certainly understood as a great sinner who through his service to Rome had disqualified himself and made himself a "heathen." To be reinstated it would not be sufficient to pray for God's mercy; he would have to leave his occupation and present satisfactory penance. The listeners thought that he was in the right place, "standing far off" and not daring to "even lift his eyes to heaven."

By juxtaposing these two figures, Jesus intended to confront his listeners with a decision. The righteousness of the pharisee and the righteousness which was accorded to the tax collector cannot be reduced to a common denominator. The righteousness of the former is not conceivable apart from an order of precedence, a comparison: "not like other men." The righteousness which the latter received through the forgiveness of God cannot, on the other hand, be subjected to any order of precedence. The order set up by the pharisees has no place for a "justified tax collector"; for the forgiven publican an order of precedence has no meaning at all. For anyone conscious of guilt there can be a question of only one authority, the ultimate.

"I tell you, this man went down to his house justified rather than the other . . ." This final judgment by Jesus must have been astounding to his hearers. Jesus knew that their rejection of sinners, in accordance with the law, did not refer to the highest authority. Jesus himself was not content with adherence to the law as such. He rather counted on God's grace as far as the neighbor was concerned. Thus he put everything on that card—and table fellowship with "sinners and publicans" was the consequence. The conflict between Jesus and the pharisees was here brought to a head.

Finally, a few words about the ninth and fourteenth verses of Luke 18, the verses which begin and end the story. The words in verse 14b—"for every one who exalts himself will be humbled, but he who humbles himself will be exalted"—were spoken by Jesus in some other context. Their placement here implies that the evangelist desired to interpret the story as a warning to the Christian community against pride and as an admonition to practice humility. The introductory verse seems to point in the same direction. When it says that the parable was addressed "to some who trusted in themselves" it implies that the pharisees were the original addressees, but it may well also have been that within the Christian community there were persons who regarded themselves as "righteous, and despised others" and who therefore needed a warning. But Jesus' story was, as we have seen, far more than a warning or an admonition.

Let us now pay attention to certain principal points presented by Robert Funk in his detailed interpretation of the parable of the great supper (Matt. 22:2–10; Luke 14:16–24). Here we have an example of the linguistic orientation evident in much contemporary scholarship. Funk shows that both of these pericopes (especially the Matthaean) have been considerably revised in the tradition. He reconstructs the original structure of the parable as follows:[22]

I. Introduction
   a. a man
   b. gives a banquet
   c. invites those (socially) worthy
II. Development and Crisis
   a. banquet is ready
   b. sends servant for courtesy reminder (in Luke once, Matthew twice)
   c. guests refuse to come and/or offer excuses, go off on pretexts (Luke three excuses, Matthew two pretexts and the response of "the rest")
III. Dénouement
   a. man is wroth
   b. invites those (socially) unworthy (Matthew once, Luke twice)
   c. table is filled
   d. judgment upon those originally invited

The language of the parable is totally neutral. It says nothing directly about what the speaker actually had in mind, nor does it indicate what the listeners could have expected him to say. The very heart of the matter is never expressly mentioned. The language of the parable is also metaphorical: it speaks of *B* when *A* is intended, thus setting the imagination in motion and calling forth a vision of that which lies behind the actual words. The parable is a model which juxtaposes two sorts of "logic," two ways of viewing and relating to reality: the one rooted in daily life and expressed in words, the other rooted in intuition, not verbalized, metaphorical.[23] A parable's "meaning" cannot be verbalized in definite statements or pronouncements. It belongs to the "logic" of statements or pronouncements that they limit, restrict, isolate, and end up in abstractions. Metaphor, on the other hand, lives within a large, vibrating context which refuses to allow itself to be reduced to statements. It intends much more than what it says. Metaphorical language preserves within itself its inherent vision and thereby includes "a world" in its pattern or its report.[24]

It is against this background that we must see Funk's interpretation of the great supper. "The parable is message (not: has a message) in the context of the ministry of Jesus."[25] In itself it says nothing beyond that which is reported. But as message it is a "linguistic aperture" onto an otherwise qualified world, and this it accomplishes without giving a hint as to who or what transforms the text. Behind it, however, Jesus stands in "half-shadow." It is he who speaks, and in the parable awakens a new world to life. It can also be said that this new world sets its mark upon Jesus' language. "In parable Jesus both witnesses to the dawn of the kingdom and brings it near . . . Jesus and his world are 'spoken' in the language of the parable."[26] But at the same time God and Jesus remain concealed—attention is directed towards man's relationship to the reality he must face. The parable is an indirect invitation to follow Jesus and settle down in this newly conjured world. The parable, moreover, does not exact a price, except insofar as it offers a world which can be received only on its own terms. "[It] is an offense to the religiously disposed ('the Pharisees'), but a joyous surprise to the religiously disinherited (the 'tax collectors and sinners')." It is like Jesus' own behavior (he ate with publicans and sinners), a rebuke of the "logic" of the pharisees but a glad message for those who possess nothing. The latter, but not the former, can accept the "logic of grace." Entrance into the new world rests upon the basis of grace. Grace is totally open; it makes no differentiations and casts out only those who themselves cast out grace—but grace does this only by offering itself for what it is. The grace which is brought about in and through the parable does not argue, gives no reasons for what it does, and does not refer to any standards by which it might be verified. It is trustworthy in itself; it is its own criterion.[27]

We shall conclude our review of the treatment of the conflict between Jesus and the pharisees by citing Dodd.

It is surprising how often the sayings of Jesus recur to this theme, of the folly and evil of self-righteousness and censoriousness. His heaviest count against the prevailing teaching of his time is precisely this: that, starting with the best intentions, it had come to encourage this folly and evil, as if it were inseparable from a high moral standard.

It is clear that there breathes through all this a lively sympathy with those whose weakness, or whose lack of opportunity, placed them at a disadvantage. But it would be misleading to regard it as nothing more than the protest of a warm-hearted, liberal-minded humanitarian. It arose out of the conviction that with the coming of the kingdom of God a new era in relations between God and man had set in. Morality might now draw directly from fresh springs. The whole apparatus of traditional regulations lost its importance.

The differences, therefore, which produced first a rift and then an irreconcilable opposition between Jesus and the dominant school of Jewish teachers in his time were not in the end . . . a matter of divergent interpretations of this or that point in the Law; . . . there is something about the antagonism, as it is reflected in the gospels, which seems to draw from an even deeper spring than apprehension of a threat to the national heritage. Jesus was charged with "blasphemy." [This] charge expresses not so much a rational judgment as a passionate, almost instinctive, revulsion of feeling against what seems to be a violation of sanctities. There must have been something about the way in which Jesus spoke and acted which provoked this kind of revulsion in minds conditioned by background, training and habit. It was this, over and above reasoned objections to certain features of his teaching, that drove the Pharisees into an unnatural (and strictly temporary) alliance with the worldly hierarchy, whose motives for pursuing Jesus to death were quite other.[28]

The Last Challenge

The final challenge faced by Jesus took place in Jerusalem, and concluded with the crucifixion. All of the gospels describe the passion history with an unparalleled fullness of detail. What is reported doubtlessly belongs to the oldest layers of tradition, but these layers have no relation to the texts as known today: the passion texts have been extensively revised and expanded in the interpretation which the primitive church gave to the suffering and death of Jesus. The original story included the entry into Jerusalem, the cleansing of the temple, the last meal with his disciples, and the account of how Jesus—at the instigation of the temple hierarchy—was condemned to death by Pilate and subsequently crucified. As we have seen,[29] Herbert Braun is skeptical about the gospels' descriptions of the last days; even other scholars of a less skeptical bent are fully conscious of the considerable uncertaintly surrounding these texts.

The first question to be faced is this: why did Jesus go to Jerusalem at Passover? Dodd suggests a carefully thought out hypothesis.[30]   As a point of departure he chooses "one of the most puzzling stories in the gospels," the account of how Jesus fed five or four thousand persons (Matthew and Mark duplicate the story). To Dodd it is probable that this incident marked the end of Jesus' activity in Galilee. During the course of the day Jesus had instructed the crowd, most likely concerning the kingdom of God, and the gathering concluded with a meal at which Jesus was the host. Varying attempts, often rationalizations, to explain the event hardly seem convincing, says Dodd, and it must be remembered that the whole account is presented as a mystery rather than a miracle. To break bread together is a sign of community, and it is certain that Jesus frequently used the picture of the festive meal to describe the realized kingdom of God. But the reaction of the crowd to his instruction and to the "sign" of the meal was totally other than Jesus had desired. Dodd holds that the Gospel of John actually preserved the memory of what happened: "they were about to come to take him by force to make him king" (John 6:15). This would have been Jesus' golden opportunity if he had chosen to be a nationalistic Messiah, but he had long since renounced such thoughts as a satanic temptation. Consistently, then, Jesus immediately sent his disciples away—"he made his disciples get into the boat and go before him to the other side" (Mark 6:45). He also managed to disperse the people peacefully. Thus the Galilean ministry came to an end, without having produced what Jesus desired and expected. The traditional nationalistic messianic expectations—reinforced by the Zealots—were so strong that Jesus' proclamation was either misunderstood or opposed.

There can hardly be any doubt as to Jesus' purpose when he took his disciples and a number of Galilean followers to Jerusalem for the Passover. His evident desire was to proclaim the kingdom of God precisely in the holy city, in the presence of the temple hierarchy, the scribes, and those who gathered to observe the holy season. This meant that he wanted to force a decision, a final stand in relation to himself and his message. Doubtlessly he was fully conscious of the risks he was taking by going, so to speak, straight into the lions' den. On the basis of the violations of the law of which he stood accused, Jesus had already—as demonstrated by Jeremias—forfeited his life.[31]

In the gospels we find three pronouncements of Jesus in which, in similar terms, he foretells his suffering, his death, and his resurrection after three days. Scholars are generally agreed that these "predictions" in their present form have been textually stylized to conform with the tradition of the early church—a standpoint adopted even by Jeremias, who otherwise tends to attach relative authenticity to such pronouncements. But at the same time these commentators do not wish to contest the fact that Jesus spoke with his disciples concerning his coming suffering. These predictions in their present form stand as pronouncements *ex eventu,* shaped after the events themselves had taken place. Not least does this pertain to the words "and be raised after three days." Nevertheless it remains reasonable to believe that Jesus' conversation in these days dealt with his immediate expectations. That in the fact of impending death he might have given up his certainty of God, his message about the kingdom of God, or his self-consciousness, is unthinkable.

Jesus' solemn entry into Jerusalem was the overture to the activities of the following days. Crowds of pilgrims prepared for Jesus a triumphal homage. The ovation with which they greeted him is rendered in various ways by the gospels. In Mark we read: "Hosanna! Blessed be he who comes in the name of the Lord!" (11:9). Matthew—like John—recalls the word of the prophet Zechariah: "Tell the daughter of Zion, Behold, your king is coming to you, humble, mounted on an ass, and on a colt, the foal of an ass" (21:5). The king who is foretold by the prophet is a king of peace: ". . . the battle bow shall be cut off, and he shall command peace to the nations" (Zech. 9:10).

The picture of the entry given by the gospels is undeniably complicated. Dodd finds no reason to doubt that Jesus entered the city upon an ass. *If* Jesus had the words of Zechariah in mind and accordingly sought an ass as his mount (which appears to have been the case, according to Matthew), the implication is that his intentions had nothing to do with nationalistic expectations and that the ass was in effect a protection against such interpretations. Yet the cries of homage which met him were ambiguous. The cry that the kingdom of David was now at hand had clear implications concerning the national destiny: it bore witness to the fact that to the bitter end Jesus was haunted by interpretations which he wanted to reject. Nevertheless the texts of the gospels themselves reveal no difference between these cries: for them Jesus was clearly the Messiah, and expressions such as "the son of David" and "the kingdom of David" can no longer be interpreted as nationalistic pretensions.

If the entry into Jerusalem was a challenge, the "cleansing of the temple" was even more so: a more demonstrative challenge can scarcely be imagined. This act of Jesus had, quite consistently, its immediate continuation in the question which Jewish authorities put to Jesus: "By what authority are you doing this . . . ?" (Mark 11:28). To drive out those who bought and sold in the temple was, to say the least, courageous. Dodd observes that "there can hardly have been any conspicuous resistance, or the garrison must have intervened to forestall a riot; it was what they were there for."[32] Jesus' act was an obvious attack against the priestly custodians of the temple. To transform the court of the temple to a marketplace—and for their own profit— was a violation of the law concerning the holiness of the temple, a law for which these custodians had responsibility. According to Roloff, Jesus snares in their own nets those whom he accuses. He says that Jesus did not intend to reform the cult or to declare that the cult should be replaced with a universal one; these are interpretations occasionally derived from the quotation from Isaiah: "My house shall be called a house of prayer for all the nations" (Mark 11:17; Isaiah 56:7). Jesus' act, in this view, is primarily an accusation to be understood as a prophetic cry for improvement. According to Roloff, Jesus could scarcely have had such an intention since in utterances of probable authenticity he also predicted the destruction of the temple.[33] It ought, however, to be pointed out that Dodd lays greater stress upon the word that the purpose of the temple was to be a house of prayer for all people: "We recall that the Son of David was popularly expected to 'cleanse Jerusalem from the Gentiles.' Jesus wanted it cleansed *for* the Gentiles."[34]

After the cleansing of the temple follows the hearing of Jesus before the hierarchy: "With what authority?" From the point of view of the authorities this question was quite legitimate. Jesus, by his actions, had attacked the basis on which the existing order rested, the law of Moses. Jesus answers with a counterquestion: "Was the baptism of

John from heaven [that is, from God] or from men?" This counter-question casts light on Jesus' intention at the cleansing of the temple (Roloff). At the baptism which he had received from John, he had come to a clear consciousness of his vocation. Jesus had often spoken of John as, through his preaching of repentance, one who was to pre-pare the way for his own proclamation of the breakthrough of the kingdom of God. If the priestly accusers acknowledged that the Bap-tist's preaching was from God, the question of Jesus' authority would thereby be answered. But when they lamely answer, "We do not know," Jesus refuses to pursue the matter any further; in other words, he contests their right to interrogate him.

We have previously seen that Herbert Braun found Jesus' counter-question concerning the Baptist to be the most exact answer which could be given to the question of authority. He says "from God" indirectly with his counterquestion—in the only way which could be understood by the opposition. In general Dodd and Braun are in complete agreement that the authority which is at stake here can only be asserted by its inherent, convincing power. Dodd writes: "The implication is that there is a kind of authority which is self-authenticat-ing; either you recognize it or you don't, and if you don't, there is nothing more to be said."[35] The temple authorities did not recognize this.

But this encounter with the temple authorities did not force Jesus into silence. He reappeared in the temple and openly attacked his opponents. "The sharp point of his attack is to be found in a parable which reads almost like a declaration of war" (in Mark 12:1–9 and parallels).[36] The first three gospels present different versions of the parable of the wicked tenant, and in all three it is apparent that the parable has been reworked within the tradition of the primitive church. One intention was evidently to refer more closely to the prophecy of Isaiah concerning the fate which was to befall Israel as the barren vineyard of the Lord; another was to make the reference to Jesus and that which was to happen to him more explicit—in other words, to strengthen the allegorizing tendency which was less clear in the para-ble's original form. Thus, for example, Mark's description of the son in the parable as "only" and "beloved" was clearly christological and natural for the early church, but it was not present in the original form of the parable. Whatever the details may be, it is nevertheless com-

78

pletely clear that in this parable Jesus pronounces a radical judgment on the leaders of Israel. The challenge has reached its climax and the result can only be arrest, judgment, and execution.

The challenger took the risk. He had counted on a violent death— as possible, as probable, as inescapable. If he had chosen to withdraw, it would have meant failure in his task as the proclaimer and representative of the kingdom of God. That which is written in Philippians, "He became obedient unto death, even death on the cross" (2:8), is an exact description of Jesus' attitude toward what lay before him. The question is one of whether we can know anything about how Jesus himself viewed his death—other than his willing acceptance of that which was to befall him as a test of his obedience. The question is, in other words: what meaning can be attributed to his suffering and death when they are viewed in the context of the kingdom of God? The material found in the Synoptic Gospels is strikingly meager. Actually there are only two categories of texts which clearly and directly refer to this question: the last supper (Mark 14:22–25 and parallels; also 1 Cor. 11:23–25), and the word about "ransom" (Mark 10:54, Matt. 20:28).

The texts about the supper have given scholars great difficulties and have led to a variety of conclusions. For the early church Jesus' death was central to its proclamation. In the oldest layers of tradition, it appears that Jesus saw his suffering foreshadowed in Isaiah's "suffering servant of the Lord," and that he thereby gave to his death a redemptive significance. In light of the great influence which the tradition of the early church exercised on the formation of the gospel texts, one can cleary understand that scholars question their authenticity on this highly sensitive point. As we remember, Braun asserts that the sacramental and ritual elements stem from Hellenistic congregations, particularly the words about bread and wine as the blood and body of Jesus.[37] His argument, however, is weakened by the fact that Hellenism had been resident in Palestine ever since Alexander the Great. Concerning the words "Take this, this is my body," Dodd says the following: "No words of his are more firmly attested."[38]

In spite of all this, however, these contrasting views are not as sharp as they might appear. No one doubts that the last meal really took place. It was celebrated as a Passover meal by Jesus and his disciples—regardless of the day on which the meal occurred (on this there is a difference of opinion between the Synoptics and John, who in this case many scholars see as being the more accurate). The meal in Jerusalem is in all cases to be understood in the context of the many meals which Jesus earlier held under the sign of the kingdom of God. If these were signs anticipating the coming fulfillment of the kingdom, so must this even more be true about the meal prior to his death. For Braun the connection of the last meal with earlier ones is a sign that the final meal had no ritual-sacramental character, an argument given credibility by the fact that the first Christian fellowship meals, the "breaking of bread" reported in Acts, lacked sacramental character and were a direct continuation of the fellowship meals which took place during Jesus' lifetime. Nor for Dodd does the last supper function directly as a sacramental "institution," and it does so even less for Jeremias. But this does not mean that the words of interpretation (to use Jeremias's phrase) which emphasize suffering lack authenticity. Jeremias reminds us that Paul, who wrote these words in the beginning of the fifth decade, says that he "received them from the Lord," which means that in any case they must have belonged to the Jesus tradition of the second decade after Jesus' death. Jeremias asserts that whereas it is hard to imagine these words of interpretation as a creation of the community, it is easy to understand them as "historical reminiscences."[39] It belonged to the Jewish Passover ritual that the father explained the meaning of the meal to his children with words of interpretation. That which is unique to the last supper "is not that Jesus 'founded' a completely new rite but that he linked an announcement and interpretation of his coming suffering with the familiar rite of grace before and after the meal."[40] The meal interprets the death of Jesus as a work of sacrifice with representative content. This self-sacrifice has, according to the one text family (Mark and Matthew), happened "for many"; according to the other family (Luke and Paul), "for you." Such an interpretation seems to have a close relation to Isaiah concerning the suffering servant of the Lord—no less than five times in Isaiah 53 does the Servant's suffering happen "for many." There can scarcely be any doubt that the passages in Isaiah had great significance for Jesus when he meditated on his own suffering and its meanings.

The words of interpretation connected with the cup give further information concerning the meaning of the words "for many" and "for you"; "the new covenant" is sealed by Jesus' sacrificial death and thereby replaces the covenant of Sinai. Dodd's view is that "he was alluding to the ancient custom by which a solemn agreement or undertaking was validated by the sacrifice of an animal." In the temple at Jerusalem the rite of animal sacrifice lingered on, but

> the language associated with it had taken on meanings proper to religion on a more developed and spiritual level. Such language is employed in the prophetic description of the Servant of the Lord who died for others; and similarly the Jewish martyrs who suffered in the time of the Maccabees were said to have offered themselves as a sacrifice for the nation. Thus the idea of sacrifice passed into that of *self*-sacrifice, as a personal and moral act. Jesus was saying that in order that the "covenant" might become effective, or in other words that the new people of God might come into existence, he was voluntarily taking a course which would lead to his death. This was the length to which he was prepared to go in identifying himself with those to whom his mission was directed. The sharing in the cup by his disciples was a demonstration of their solidarity with their Master, both as beneficiaries of his sacrifice, and as being themselves committed to a like self-devotion for others. . . .[41]

Even if the core of the texts concerning the last supper is within reach, it can still not be denied that these texts contain significantly uncertain elements and cause questions which have no categorical answers. Luke preserves most of the original narrative character—in the other gospels, liturgical stylization is more evident.

Finally, a word concerning "ransom." The text in Mark is as follows: "For the Son of man also came not to be served but to serve, and to give his life as a ransom for many" (10:45). "Ransom" or "ransom money" was given for slaves to be set free, for ground and land, and so on. There are different opinions as to the authenticity of this word. According to Braun it stems from the theology of the community; the parallel text in Luke (22:27) speaks only about service, and is understood by many as the original text.[42] Jeremias, and others with him, defend the authenticity of the Marcan passage. He finds that in Mark the title "Son of man" has a secondary significance, but concludes that Luke and Mark have built on different Palestinian traditions with two divergent views concerning the content of the word "ransom."[43]

For obvious reasons, interpretations of the gospel texts which deal with Jesus' view of his suffering run the risk of reading into the text attitudes which stem from the primitive church's understanding—

Pauline, Johannine, and other—of Jesus' death. Nor is it out of the realm of possibility that views from a much later theology can be smuggled in, lending their color to that which is said.

Notes

1. C. H. Dodd, *The Founder of Christianity* (New York: Macmillan, and London: Collier-Macmillan, 1970), p. 57.
2. Norman Perrin, *Rediscovering the Teaching of Jesus* (New York: Harper & Row, and London: SCM, 1967), pp. 67ff. For further developments in the work of Perrin see *A Modern Pilgrimage in New Testament Christology* (Philadelphia: Fortress, 1974) and *Jesus and the Language of the Kingdom: Symbol and Metaphor in New Testament Interpretation* (Philadelphia: Fortress, and London: SCM, 1976). Perrin's work has been especially important in the advancement of study of the Gospel of Mark, the problem of the "Son of man" title, and the question of New Testament language.
3. Amos N. Wilder, *The Language of the Gospel: Early Christian Rhetoric* (New York: Harper & Row, and London: SCM, 1964), pp. 73, 74, 71, 76. A revised edition of this book was published as *Early Christian Rhetoric: The Language of the Gospel* (Cambridge: Harvard University Press, 1971).
4. Joachim Jeremias, *New Testament Theology: The Proclamation of Jesus*, trans. John Bowden (New York: Scribner's, and London: SCM, 1971), p. 117; cf. also Perrin, *Rediscovering the Teaching of Jesus*, pp. 102ff.
5. Jürgen Roloff, *Das Kerygma und der irdische Jesus* (Göttingen: Vandenhoeck & Ruprecht, 1970), pp. 223ff.
6. Cf. Birger Gerhardsson, "Geistiger Opferdienst nach Matth. 6, 1–6, 16–21," *Neues Testament und Geschichte*, ed. Heinrich Baltensweiler and Bo Reicke (Zürich / Tübingen: Theologischer Verlag / J. C. B. Mohr [Paul Siebeck], 1972).
7. Roloff, *Das Kerygma und der irdische Jesus*, p. 227.
8. Herbert Braun, *Jesus* (Stuttgart: Kreuz, 1969), p. 145.
9. C. H. Dodd, *The Parables of the Kingdom*, rev. ed., trans. S. H. Hooke (New York: Scribner's, 1961). The first edition, 1935, is available from Welwyn Garden City: Nisbet.; Joachim Jeremias, *The Parables of Jesus*, 3d rev. ed. (New York: Scribner's, and London: SCM, 1972); Wilder, *The Language of the Gospel* (see note 3); Eta Linnemann, *Jesus of the Parables: Introduction and Exposition*, trans. John Sturdy (New York: Harper & Row, and London: S.P.C.K., 1966); Dan O. Via, Jr., *The Parables: Their Literary and Existential Dimension* (Philadelphia: Fortress, 1967).
10. Wilder, *The Language of the Gospel*, p. 81; cf. Harald Riesenfeld, "The Parables in the Synoptic and in the Johannine Traditions," *The Gospel Tradition*, trans. Margaret Rowley and Robert Kraft (Philadelphia: Fortress, and Oxford: Basil Blackwell, 1970), pp. 139–69.
11. Via, *The Parables*, pp. 2–107.

12. Robert W. Funk, *Language, Hermeneutic, and Word of God: The Problem of Language in the New Testament and Contemporary Theology* (New York: Harper & Row, 1966).

13. K. H. Rengstorf, *Die Re-Investitur des Verlorenen Sohnes in der Gleichniserzählung Jesus Luk. 15:11–32* (Köln and Opladen: Veroffentlichungen der Arbeitsgemeinschaft für Forschung des Landes Nordrhein-Westfalen—Geisteswissenschaften 137, 1967).

14. Via, *The Parables*, pp. 162–76.

15. Linnemann, *Jesus of the Parables*, p. 75.

16. Rengstorf, *Die Re-Investitur des Verlorenen Sohnes*, pp. 21 ff.

17. C. H. Dodd, *The Founder of Christianity*, p. 60.

18. Norman Perrin, *Rediscovering the Teaching of Jesus*, pp. 94–101.

19. Via, *The Parables*, p. 171.

20. Ibid., p. 174.

21. Rengstorf, *Die Re-Investitur des Verlorenen Sohnes*, pp. 27–69.

22. Funk, *Language, Hermeneutic, and Word of God*, p. 165–66.

23. Ibid., pp. 193–97.

24. Ibid., pp. 142–43.

25. Ibid., p. 196.

26. Ibid., p. 197.

27. Ibid., pp. 196–97.

28. C. H. Dodd, *The Founder of Christianity*, pp. 76–79.

29. Cf. p. 20 above.

30. Dodd, *The Founder of Christianity*, pp. 131ff.

31. Jeremias, *The Parables of Jesus*, pp. 278ff.

32. Dodd, *The Founder of Christianity*, p. 145.

33. Roloff, *Das Kerygma und der irdische Jesus*, pp. 89–102.

34. Dodd, *The Founder of Christianity*, p. 147.

35. Ibid., p. 148.

36. Ibid., p. 149.

37. Braun, *Jesus*, pp. 76–77.

38. Dodd, *The Founder of Christianity*, p. 109.

39. Jeremias, *The Parables of Jesus*, p. 289.

40. Ibid., p. 290.

41. Dodd, *The Founder of Christianity*, p. 109.

42. Braun, *Jesus*, p. 142.

43. Jeremias, *The Parables of Jesus*, p. 298.

4

JESUS AND THOSE AROUND HIM

The Appeal

In the second chapter we came to terms with Jesus' radical ethical proclamation based on "love for God," realized in and through "love for neighbor." The main theme of the third chapter was Jesus' unconditional acceptance of "sinners and publicans," an attitude which was highly offensive to the Jews of his time; this behavior reached its climax in his granting forgiveness of sins, an act reserved to God alone. It may seem as though these two attitudes were irreconcilable; we recall that Braun as well as Gerhardsson described this combination of radical demand and lavish generosity as highly unique, meaning that this combination of seeming opposites is quite peculiar to Jesus and characteristic of his association with people. It goes without saying that we ought not to expect a theoretical treatment of this theme in the gospels. The textual accounts concerning Jesus' actual treatment of the people who followed him shed ample light on the connection between his radical demand and lavish generosity. We shall first deal with the appeal Jesus makes to his contemporaries.

In the first chapter of Mark, it says: "The time is fulfilled and the kingdom of God is at hand; repent and believe in the gospel." We are hardly dealing with authentic words of Jesus; it is a summary, either by the tradition or by the evangelist, of the appeal made by Jesus. His message that the kingdom of God is at hand was also an admonition to take a stand, to make a decision for or against it. If such an admonition was latent in, for example, the parable of the prodigal son, we encounter it directly and with unmistakable clarity in parables such as the invitation to the great supper or the two sons, the one who said *yes* and did not go to work in the vineyard, and the other who said *no*, but repented and went (Matt. 21:28–32). Basically all of Jesus' proclamation, that which was direct as well as that which made use of parables as a means of instruction, placed men before a decision, which demanded an answer which could either be *yes* or *no*. How was that appeal received?

Before this question can be answered, it is necessary to take a look at the situation in the country. Scholars agree that the situation was critical. We might do well to listen to Dodd: "The condition of Judea in the first century was pathological. It was torn with faction; a largely secularized priesthood furthered its own ambitions by subservience to the foreign power; the mass of the people seethed with impotent hatred of Rome. The efforts of good and devoted religious teachers had the effect of widening the breach between the pious and the despised 'people of the land.'"[1] The situation was characterized by desperation and at the same time by high expectations. This fire of expectancy was richly nourished by flourishing apocalyptic literature, which painted with fantastic imagery the transformation which was immediately to take place: a messianic kingdom of David would put an end to the present chaos and give Israel new greatness.

In Jesus' proclamation of the coming kingdom of God there is a fierce consciousness of the seriousness of the situation and of the danger threatening the Jewish people. In clear words he lets the leaders of the people know that they are not able to "interpret the signs of the time" (Matt. 16:3). He interprets them himself—as did the prophets—as threats of impending destruction and ruin. Nevertheless, behind the words of judgment and the cries of lamentation there is a deep melancholy: "Jerusalem . . . how often would I have gathered your children together as a hen gathers her brood under her wings and you would not" (Matt. 23:37).

We can now return to the question of who the people who gathered around Jesus were. His critics were inclined to say "sinners and publicans"—those were their words of abuse. Such religiously- and socially-ostracized people no doubt belonged to Jesus' followers, although they were only a small minority. The great majority, however, came from the despised "people of the land." When followers of this kind are mentioned in the gospels as "poor" and "simple," Jeremias believes that the descriptions originally stem from Jesus' critics as expressions of their disdain.[2] For Jesus, though, they became words of honor—for example, when he set the poor against the rich (Luke 6:20, 24) and the simple against "the wise and understanding" (Matt.

11:25). God's kingdom belonged to the poor, and that which had been concealed to the wise was now revealed to the babes.

The innermost circle of those who followed Jesus was made up of the disciples whom he himself had called and chosen, "the twelve." They had left "everything" and followed Jesus. These disciples were given private instruction by Jesus and were also entrusted with the task, as his special messengers, to preach the urgent gospel of the coming kingdom of God. Among Jesus' immediate followers there were also a few women who "served them with their possessions"—they must have been widows, since no other women had the right to dispose of their own property.

When Jesus gathered people around him in this way, he created a new community. He was not the only one who tried to accomplish this. The same can to a certain extent be said about the pharisees, and to a greater extent about the Qumran sect. But it was not Jesus' intention to create a new sect; his was a totally open community without entrance exams. Nevertheless, it did have its own characteristics, chiefly directed toward the coming kingdom of God. This was no abstract ideal for Jesus. Just as "loving God" should be realized through "loving one's neighbor," so the kingdom of God would take shape in the world of men, and it was this that was prepared for in and through the community around Jesus, the new "eschatological" beginning of God's people. The kingdom started in Israel, to be sure, but a universal perspective was inherent from the outset.

In the gospels we encounter this motif of community in varying expressions and images. We can disregard the fact that on a few occasions the word *ecclesia* is mentioned. It has been contested that these texts could be authentic; in any case there could have been no question of a "church" in the sense that this word has subsequently taken. Other expressions are more important: the picture of the shepherd and sheep, the reference to the new covenant foretold by the prophets, and, not least, the community gathered around Jesus as God's household (Matt. 10:25) or as the family whose members are Jesus' "brothers and sisters" (Mark 3:35 and parallels). Jeremias says, in a pronouncement which he himself describes as being extremely sharp, that "the only significance of the whole of Jesus' activity is to gather the eschatological people of God."[3] At any rate it is clear that Jesus wanted to create a community, and that this, let us say, the community of the period of waiting was conceived as an anticipation of that which was to come. The table-fellowship which, as we have seen, played such an important role in the community of Jesus clearly attests to this.

Those who had been incorporated into this community had thus answered *yes* to Jesus' appeal. The appeal speaks of "repentance" and "conversion." What meaning do these words have? Earlier we noted an "unconditional" acceptance on the part of Jesus. Does not "repentance" imply very definite conditions? Such an interpretation is surely appropriate if one considers what has happened in the history of the church. When Dodd broaches the subject, he speaks of the word "repent" as most nearly meaning "to be sorry for your sins." But this, he says,

> is not what the Greek word *metanoia* means. It means quite simply to think again, to have second thoughts, to change your mind. "Repentance" as the gospels mean it is a readjustment of ideas and emotions, from which a new pattern of life and behavior will grow (as the "fruit of repentance"). . . . "Unless you turn around and become like children, you will never enter the kingdom of God"; or, in other words, "Whoever does not accept the kingdom of God like a child will never enter it." This "turning around" is a large part of what is meant by "repentance" in the gospels. It is learning to think of God as your Father and of yourself as his child, quite simply: . . . [to accept] goodness beyond justice.[4]

It may be of interest to take a look at a few interpretations of this passage about the children. According to Perrin we are dealing here with one of the most pregnant of Jesus' words; the stress is on God's activity resulting in an answer of spontaneity and trust.[5] For Braun, the reference to the children as examples is something highly "un-Jewish"—it involves the child's ability to accept a gift spontaneously, without second thoughts and calculations.[6] For Jeremias the reference to the child implies the ability confidently to say *abba* to God.[7] The decisive motive behind "repentance" in Jesus—in contrast to the Baptist—is the "experience of the incomprehensible goodness of God. Repentance springs from grace. God's goodness is the only power that can really lead a man to repentance." Therefore a note of joy will sound throughout Jesus' descriptions of what repentance is all about: it is to put on the wedding garment (Matt. 22:11), to anoint one's head with oil when fasting (Matt. 6:11). "Repentance is joy that God is so gracious. Even more, repentance is *God's* joy."[8]

Scholars describe "repentance" in different ways, but the essential point remains the same for all of them: namely, the acceptance of the gift which is being offered unconditionally. Jesus does not make any demands that must first be fulfilled; he does not question man concerning his sins, he does not test his penance, and not a word is said about man having to demonstrate qualifications which would make him acceptable. It is solely a question of whether one accepts the fact that one is accepted—because of God's goodness, which exceeds all justice and which receives with open arms.

But this preaching about repentance was offensive to the pattern of living which the scribes and pharisees had shaped. It most certainly was also their main task to refer to God's mercy and goodness, to the God who forgives. But the "logic of grace," to quote Funk, which characterized Jesus' activity, was alien to them and seemed to them incompatible with their guardianship of the "logic of the law." To leave every thought about one's own qualifications aside was in their eyes a much too easy and broad way—while in reality, the total surrendering of the self before the grace of God was the narrow gate which led to life (Matt. 7:13).

Those who rejected Jesus did not believe in the message he preached; in contrast, those who joined him must have believed it in some form or other. We must thus face the question of what the Synoptic Gospels mean by *faith*. One might expect that what is said here about faith would have been strongly influenced by the primitive church's understanding of faith in Christ, but nothing can conceal the fact that "faith" here has a different profile than it was to have later. Jesus nowhere demands faith in himself, either as the Messiah or with reference to any other title of high honor used by the primitive church. There is no direct speech about faith in his message. In Matthew there are, to be sure, two occasions on which faith "in Jesus" is mentioned—"one of these little ones who believe in me" (18:6) and "believe in him" (27:42)—but on textual grounds these expressions do not correspond to the Marcan parallels and must be regarded as additions by Matthew.[9]

The number of passages in which words about faith occurs in the Synoptic Gospels is relatively limited. More than half of them are related to Jesus' healing miracles. It seems natural to assume that "faith" in this instance means trust in Jesus' ability to help. Such faith

Jesus also found outside of Judaism: in a Samaritan leper, in a Canaanite woman, and in a Roman officer. Roloff has given careful attention to the meaning of "faith" in connection with the healing miracles: to what extent did those who had been healed understand that the healing was a question of important "signs"? For example, when one of the ten lepers who had been healed returns to Jesus in order to praise God and is received with the words "your faith has saved you," Jesus' words mean that this man in his encounter with Jesus as healer has experienced God's *heilvolle* presence. The point of the story, then, is that although all ten have been healed, only one has understood the significance of the healing as a "sign." Roloff seems here to have somewhat overinterpreted the event he analyzes.[10]

In respect to Jesus' healing the ill, faith is attached to definite acts. It has been made concrete in the actual encounter with him, and thereby appears as something to a certain degree limited to specific points in time. Roloff makes this point in order to describe how the meaning of faith is somewhat different in respect to the disciples themselves. A fellowship between Jesus and the disciples is *presupposed*, and the question concerning the disciples' faith is whether they hold on to and preserve this fellowship, and if in their daily living they meet the demands which are made of them. The results vary: we are told of their successful deeds as messengers of Jesus, but also of their shortcomings. Time and again Jesus must scold them for their weak faith— in Mark their "unbelief," in Matthew their "little faith."

Even though Jesus does not speak directly about the message he preaches—as Mark does in his summary: "Believe in the gospel" (1:15) —all of his proclamation is nonetheless an appeal to trust in the power of God's goodness. In this context Jesus' paradoxical imagery of the power of faith must be understood. Faith moves mountains (Matt. 17:20): "If you had faith as a grain of mustard seed, you could say to this sycamine tree, 'Be rooted up, and planted in the sea'" (Luke 17:6). Jesus uses such images to demonstrate the overwhelming power that little faith alone (the little mustard seed) possesses. What Jesus intended was not "spectacular miracles" but rather the destruction of the demonic power of evil which would occur in the coming kingdom of God. He also recognized and gave his help to those of weak faith who sought his help, even to the father who in his anxiety cried out in words which, according to Jeremias, ought to be translated: "I believe, help me in spite of my unbelief" (Mark 9:24).[11]

Jesus' Lifestyle

The acceptance given by Jesus to those who answered his appeal affirmatively put them in a totally new situation in life. They became free, redressed, lifted up into a new sphere. In Jesus' proclamation and work they had met the God who in his overwhelming goodness forgives sins, the God of the lost. Their lives had been given integrity and a new responsibility. We find in the gospels descriptions of how Jesus turns to individuals and cares for them. His purpose, however, was not to pick out single individuals, but rather to create a new community "worthy of the name of the people of God" (Dodd), a people living under the sign of the kingdom of God which was breaking through. This community of Jesus was by no means an exclusive club; it was open to all who wanted to join.

None are excluded from the community but those who willingly leave it and thus exclude themselves (Göran Forkman).[12] The rules which in Matthew are offered for the treatment of erring brethren and which even describe exclusion from the "church" do not stem from the earthly Jesus: "The situation does not fit into the life of Jesus and the words do not fit into his mouth." These rules had their origin in the primitive tradition and in Matthew they have been given a formulation characteristic of his gospel.

But if the community of Jesus thus lacks fixed boundaries and can most nearly be described as fluid, does this not mean that it exists as an indefinite and contourless entity? On the contrary, it has an unmistakable and substantial lifestyle of its own. To be in the community involves responsibility. The gift which was given was an outright gift, but it could not be kept if it was not used—it could not be a talent hidden in the ground (Matt. 25:14–30) without being lost. The forgiveness which was bestowed was whole and pure, but it could not be kept if the one who had been forgiven did not show limitless willingness to forgive his fellow men. This is a theme which, time and again, meets us in the gospels—suffice it to mention the fifth petition in the Our Father, and the parable of the servant who had been released from his thousand talents, yet who did not hesitate to demand from his fellow servant the one hundred denarii owed him (Matt. 18:28). When Peter asks if it is enough to forgive an erring brother seven times, the answer, "not seven times, but seventy times seven," did not mean four hundred and ninety, but unlimited willingness to forgive (Matt. 18:21–22). These words about the obligations of forgiveness are random examples of Jesus' ethical instruction, which was intended first of all for his immediate disciples but which by no means concerned them only. The community of Jesus was given its specific characteristics by the unity of radical grace and radical demand.

There may be reason to return and consider further what meaning and scope the "law" had in Jesus' authoritative ethical teaching. Albert Schweitzer, who saw Jesus from the perspective of "thoroughgoing eschatology"—or rather "thoroughgoing apocalypticism"—described Jesus' ethic as an "interim ethic," shaped with reference to the immediate end-time of all things. Schweitzer's view resonated among scholars, but was not maintained in the long run. Davies writes: "Even if Jesus did contemplate the End of all things to come, this in itself was not the secret of his illumination."[13] This well describes the position of contemporary scholars towards Schweitzer's "interim ethic." It is a view reinforced by the fact that Jesus' ethical proclamation had clear reference to the "law" which was concentrated in the central confession of Israel, the *Shema*. Jesus' interpretation of the *Shema* to mean that "love of God" was to be realized in and through "love of one's neighbor" was certainly no interim ethic.

When Matthew in the Sermon on the Mount gathered some of the pronouncements which Jesus had made on different occasions and shaped and interpreted them in view of the situation in the primitive church, he was seeing Jesus as a lawgiver alongside Moses, but of a higher dignity. This view puts us before two questions: one concerns the authority of Jesus, and the other concerns the meaning of the word "law" in Jesus' proclamation.

For Matthew, Jesus is sanctioned as a lawgiver by the authority he possesses as the Messiah. Yet this is Matthew's and the primitive church's interpretation. Jesus himself, in contrast, refers neither to any messiahship nor to any honorific title. He attaches his ethical demand to his proclamation of the coming kingdom of God and speaks of these two matters with sovereign self-assurance, without reference to any authority, and without hesitation concerning the will of God. To quote Davies: "He himself in his own intuitive awareness of the will of God is the source of the radical ethic."[14]

The question concerning what was "the most important in the law" was no problem to Jesus. His approach to the legal texts was quite other than that of the scribes. To him it was basically not a question of firm commands, or of law in the usual sense of the word, but of fundamental demands and a lifestyle. He was preoccupied with neither a strict observance of the law nor detailed obedience to fixed legal texts. In reality, therefore, it is erroneous to describe him as a lawgiver—he was that in neither his contemporaries' sense of the word nor in the current sense of the word. Jesus makes an all-inclusive demand for constant care for one's neighbor. How this is to be applied in particular cases is ultimately up to each individual. The responsibility is one's own. The so-called golden rule demonstrates this: "So whatever you wish that men would do to you, do so to them" (Matt. 7:12). Jesus' question also proves this: "And why do you not judge for yourselves what is right?" (Luke 12:57). Such words are clearly of fundamental importance. They must have sounded completely foreign to those who observed the law.

Was Jesus' radical ethic, his radical demand, only intended for his community? It can be answered that it was his intention to proclaim that which was the will of God the Creator; the perspective was universal. In the gospels there are a great many indications which confirm this: Jesus derived the demand for the indissolubility of marriage directly from the will of the Creator, which was given from the "very beginning." To act in accordance with the will of God was not possible only for the followers of Jesus; the parable of the good Samaritan presents an outsider fulfilling the divine will. The interpretation of the judgment of "the King" (Matt. 25) involves problems to which we shall return later, but one thing seems clear: those who are called "blessed by my Father" come from "all people." Those who belong to the community of Jesus have, like the chosen people of Israel, no certainty of being judged righteous, and even those who claim to have prophesied and done mighty works in his name can be rejected (Matt. 7:22–23).

In the lifestyle of the community of Jesus, one can speak of the imitation of God and of Jesus. Dodd observes that the imitation of God is not by itself unique to the gospels. Such a demand can be "found in both Jewish and Greek moralists of the period." The question then becomes what it is that is to be *imitated*. It may, for example, be an ideal of holiness which remains quite passive in relation to man and the world. But "in the best Jewish teaching (going back to the prophets of the Old Testament) the attributes of God which are to be imitated are those which can be conceived on the analogy of human virtues at their highest; such as his even-handed justice, his mercy, his faithfulness."[15] Jeremias points out that the words "Be merciful, even as your Father is merciful" (Luke 6:36) have direct parallels within Judaism (in the parallel passage, Matthew 5:48, where Luke has "merciful," the word which has been translated as "perfect" most nearly means wholehearted, intact, undivided in relation to God as well as to one's neighbor).[16] When Jesus speaks of imitating God, the emphasis is on "the undiscriminating generosity and sympathy of the heavenly Father, particularly as shown towards those who are unworthy of it. . . .To love God is to live as his child; to live as a child of God is to treat your neighbor as God treats you."[17]

The question of what it meant to follow Jesus is more complicated, since we are dealing here with two different categories of people: on the one hand, the disciples who "left all" in order literally to follow Jesus, who were given private instruction by him and were entrusted with special tasks—and on the other hand, all who listened to him, attached themselves to him, and thus became disciples in a more general sense. It is evident that discipleship in the former case has a specific meaning, but it is at the same time dangerous to set up boundaries between what Jesus said to these disciples and what he "said to all" (Luke 9:23).

Discipleship is intimately bound to "fellowship with Jesus." The lifestyle is made concrete in that Jesus functions as the example and source of inspiration. Birger Gerhardsson has, on good grounds, stressed the role which Israel's central confession, the *Shema*, played in Jesus' own life and teachings.[18] It is not surprising that the words "imitate Jesus" reflect Jesus' interpretation of what it means to "love God with all one's heart, with all one's soul and with all one's might." To "imitate Jesus" (*imitatio*) does not mean what we usually think of as "imitation." It is not a repetition of Jesus' actual deeds, but in varying situations to obey God by serving one's neighbor, with Jesus standing as the unattainable example.

"With all one's heart" means wholehearted obedience to God and his will; the striking feature of Jesus' interpretation is that such obedience is to be realized in relation to one's neighbor. The consequence of this is that because obedience to God is at the center, man is at the center. Jesus sets an example in that he has "come to serve." To serve becomes the word above all other words—it is the sign of the lifestyle. In this service there are no superfluous acts, no so-called extra deeds: "When you have done all that is commanded to you, say, 'We are unworthy servants; we have only done what was our duty'" (Luke 17:10). Here belong the many words concerning hearing *and* doing, and of "bearing fruit." To hear, to listen in all seriousness, is the presupposition for doing, but the stress is on doing. The criticism of those who listen without doing is sharp: they exclude themselves from fellowship with Jesus, and then it is of no avail for them to say "Lord, Lord" (Matt. 7:21; cf. Luke 6:46). The one who does the will of God is Jesus' "brother and sister, and mother" (Matt. 12:50 and parallels).

"With all your soul" implies willingness to humble oneself, to suffer, and if necessary to sacrifice one's own life. It is evident that this is a prominent motif in the lifestyle of those who are in fellowship with Jesus, and that we are here dealing with words which Jesus addressed "to all." A key passage in this context is Luke 9:23: "And he said to all, If any man would come after me, let him deny himself and take up the cross daily and follow me." The word "daily," according to many scholars, is clearly secondary. It is a parenthetic reinterpretation, which is nevertheless instructive since it shows that the words about taking up the cross have not exclusively been conceived as referring to martyrdom—"daily" does not fit into *that* context. The theme which we encounter here and which recurs with different variations is undeniably a main theme in Jesus' teaching: the one who wants to save his life will lose it, and the one who loses himself will save his life. To want to save one's life means to become the center around which everything moves, while to lose oneself means to serve without restrictions; in one case "saving" actually means losing, and in the other, "losing" actually means finding. This was the lifestyle which concerned "all."

"With all your might"—"might" most nearly refers to earthly power and property; might and mammon belong together. Jesus' attitude toward this power involves a radical re-evaluation of values.[19] Gathering treasures on earth "where moth and rust consume" is contrasted to gathering treasures in heaven (Matt. 6:19–21). God is set against mammon: "No one can serve two masters . . . you cannot serve God and mammon" (Matt. 6:24). If mammon becomes Lord, he becomes Lord in place of God. When Jesus speaks concerning the dangers of wealth, as he often does, he speaks to the point.

The words of Jesus concerning wealth do, to be sure, remain problematic. The story of his encounter with a certain rich young man (Mark 10:17–22; Matt. 19:16–22; Luke 18:18–23) is clearly interpreted in Luke's version as that to all who would follow him Jesus presented a demand for a total renunciation of property (although Jeremias suggests that in its oldest form the encounter was a direct invitation to the man to follow Jesus in the manner of the "twelve," rather than a more general call to discipleship).[20] Further, that very story is in Matthew followed by Jesus' well-known words that it is easier for a camel to go through the needle's eye than it is for someone of wealth to enter the kingdom of God. Yet, on the other hand, the gospels indicate that Jesus had many disciples—in the broadest sense of that word—who were never asked to become unpropertied: Martha and Mary, Zaccheus, and others. Under all circumstances, though, it remained of chief importance that disciples of all kinds be liberated from attachment to mammon, from coveteousness and avarice, and that they be willing to share their possessions in service to their neighbors—and in that regard, care for the poor had the highest priority.

Notes

1. C. H. Dodd, *The Founder of Christianity* (New York: Macmillan, and London: Collier-Macmillan, 1970), pp. 85ff.

2. Joachim Jeremias, *New Testament Theology,* trans. John Bowden (New York: Scribner's, and London: SCM, 1971), p. 111.

3. Ibid., p. 170.

4. Dodd, *The Founder of Christianity,* pp. 58–62.

5. Norman Perrin, *Rediscovering the Teaching of Jesus* (New York: Harper & Row, and London: SCM, 1967), p. 146.

6. Herbert Braun, *Jesus* (Stuttgart: Kreuz, 1969), pp. 69, 86.

7. Jeremias, *New Testament Theology,* p. 157.

8. Ibid., p. 158.

9. Ibid., p. 162.

10. Jürgen Roloff, *Das Kerygma und der irdische Jesus* (Göttingen: Vandenhoeck & Ruprecht, 1970), pp. 152ff.

11. Jeremias, *New Testament Theology*, p. 166.

12. Göran Forkman, *The Limits of the Religious Community* (Lund: Gleerups, 1972), pp. 124–32.

13. W. D. Davies, *The Sermon on the Mount* (Cambridge: Cambridge University Press, 1966), p. 144.

14. Ibid., p. 148.

15. Dodd, *The Founder of Christianity*, pp. 64–65.

16. Jeremias, *New Testament Theology*, p. 212.

17. Dodd, *The Founder of Christianity*, p. 65.

18. Cf. pp. 41ff. above.

19. Braun, *Jesus*, p. 35.

20. Jeremias, *New Testament Theology*, pp. 222–23.

5

THE KINGDOM OF GOD
AND ITS REPRESENTATIVE

The Kingdom of God—Present and Future

The account of contemporary Jesus research which has been given in the three previous chapters has in important aspects led to a historically trustworthy picture of the earthly Jesus. This does not mean, of course, that anyone has been able to determine in detail which words or deeds are authentic. Nor does it mean that the different scholars do not vary in their positions and conclusions. In the second chapter, however, we were able to arrive at a clear picture of what Jesus demands in relation to God and one's fellow man; we have seen how everything is concentrated in an attitude in which "love" is the determining factor, an attitude in which "love of God" is realized in and through "love of one's neighbor." In comparison with this central and radical demand, all other demands are secondary. In the third and fourth chapters we have laid bare the essential elements of Jesus' association with people, both in respect to his encounter with the leaders of contemporary Judaism and his relation to the disciples who followed him, the community of Jesus. In both cases everything revolved around the kingdom of God, which he proclaimed was near at hand. It is evident that he was not only the herald of this kingdom, but that he also functioned on its behalf.

When, in this chapter, we deal in greater detail with "the kingdom of God and its representative," we will encounter wider differences among the scholars. This pertains especially to such problems as Jesus' attitude to contemporary Jewish apocalyptic and the importance which such titles as "Messiah" and "Son of man" may have had for him. Here we find problems which were controversial during the earlier part of twentieth-century scholarship, and which are still of interest—but which will perhaps never be solved definitively.

Concerning the question of apocalyptic, we recall that Albert

Schweitzer advocated a "thoroughgoing eschatology." This term scarcely reflects Schweitzer's actual viewpoint, for in reality he described Jesus as a "thoroughgoing apocalyptic." According to Schweitzer, Jesus described the imminent kingdom of God in the loud colors of current apocalyptic, and the "ethic" which he proclaimed was totally determined by the apocalyptic vision and hence stood as an interim ethic, a provisional ethic. Schweitzer's position had wide influence, not least within the early form-critical movement. As an antithesis to this point of view, C. H. Dodd, early in the 1930s, offered an interpretation which he described as "realized eschatology." This expression is also problematic, inasmuch as there is undeniably a certain tension between the two words. But Dodd's intention is clear; he wants to move the stress from the apocalyptic to that which is "realized" in Jesus' word and deed. Dodd sees this as the essential factor, even though it also includes an eschatological element, even in a future sense. When Dodd thus accents the present (that which is realized in Jesus' activity), he does not question any more than other contemporary scholars the fact that Jesus expected the breaking in of the kingdom of God in all its fullness within the near future.

But before we deal more closely with the different tenses, present and future, we shall first look back and think somewhat in the past perfect tense. Jesus was not the first to speak about the kingdom of God. This fact is stressed not least by Gerhardsson in his polemic against Schweitzer's "one-sided cultivation" of the "eschatological" perspective. This is certainly an important perspective, but one must not overlook the fact that Jesus, when speaking of the kingdom of God, does so "in reference to an inherited ideology . . . the kingdom of God is something which was and has been."[1] The Old Testament also speaks of the kingdom of God: "Thy kingdom is an everlasting kingdom, and thy dominion endures throughout generations" (Psalm 145:13). This view of God was essential for Jesus; it was the natural background for his own proclamation of the kingdom of God. That which has happened, that which God has done in the past, is a presupposition for that which is now taking place and is about to take place. That which is now taking place, on one hand, is a continuation and a fulfillment; on the other, it is something totally new.

Many scholars maintain that our Western translations of the Hebrew *malkuth shamajim* and its Aramaic equivalent do not cover the meaning of the original. When in translation one speaks of the kingdom of God, the reign of God, the dominion of God, the rule of God, *Gottes Reich, Gottes Königsherrschaft, le Royaume de Dieu,* and so forth, such formulations seem altogether too abstract in relation to what the original intended—this is even true of the expression "reign of God" which is usually considered a better translation than the "kingdom of God." If one wants to discover what is present in the original but lacking in the Western words, one should return to Psalm 145. When it speaks of "the kingdom of God," it combines this word with God's "mighty deeds," his "great work." This means that "the kingdom of God" is conceived of as something *dynamic*—one cannot speak of this "kingdom" without immediately thinking of God's activity and his "deeds." One thinks concretely, not abstractly.

This is also, to a great extent, Jesus' point of view, when he speaks about both that which is taking place and that which will take place when the kingdom of God comes "with power" (Mark 9:1). Just as God above all had acted in the past in the history of Israel—the exodus, Mount Sinai—so he is now about to act decisively and definitively. Jesus' proclamation of the coming of the kingdom of God has precisely such content. What is involved is the present as well as the future. The present means that the powers of the coming kingdom of God are now at work, made known in Jesus' words and ministry. God acts, using Jesus as his tool: "But if it is by the finger of God that I cast out demons, then the kingdom of God has come upon you" (Luke 11:20). Jesus expects that the kingdom of God will appear within the near future "with power," but it is already at work wherever he functions as its representative. We have previously acquainted ourselves with this representative function of Jesus, and we need only here recall a few essentials: healing the sick, forgiving sins, being with and eating with the lost and rejected, gathering people about him and making them members of his community.

There is, however, reason to dwell on a few matters which shed light on the relation between that which is and that which is to come. Our concern is both the role which the motif of struggle plays and the question of man's possibility of seeing and experiencing in the present what belongs basically to the coming kingdom of God.

The decisive—one could say the eschatologically decisive—struggle for the coming kingdom of God has begun. Jesus is engaged in a war against demonic powers, against the reign of Satan. We have already touched upon this when speaking about exorcism;[2] we shall now view it from the point of view of the kingdom of God. The conception of "demons" was, to be sure, commonplace within contemporary Judaism. The characteristic thing for Jesus, as Jeremias expresses it, was that he did not look "atomistically" at the power of evil: it is concentrated in Satan, and the demons, "the evil spirits," are conceived of as soldiers in "the power of the enemy" (Luke 10:19). Satan stands as the representative of the collective power of evil. He is the destroyer of creation; he is the enemy. He is the enemy who sows weeds in the field of the kingdom of God (Matt. 13:25–28). Jesus enters into a duel with him; he is strong and "well armed," but Jesus is stronger, conquers him, and "divides his spoil" (Luke 11:21). That which is taking place is seen by Jesus as the beginning of victory over Satan's power, and in a vision Jesus sees Satan fall (Luke 10:18). The evil spirits are powerless before him, and Satan is about to be disarmed. There is, writes Jeremias, "no analogy to these statements in contemporary Judaism; neither the synagogue nor Qumran knows anything of a vanquishing of Satan that is already beginning in the present."[3] This drastic imagery confirms that the decisive struggle for the coming kingdom of God has been launched and is now in full operation, that the *dynamis* of the kingdom of God, its power, is at work—now.

The role that Satan plays has no counterpart in the Old Testament. There he is conceived of as a "prosecutor" whom God can use—as in the case of Job—to put men to the test. The same point of view also appears in certain instances in the New Testament. In the account of the temptations of Jesus, Jesus is brought out in the desert to be tempted by Satan; the Passion story reads: "Satan demanded to have you, that he might sift you like wheat" (Luke 22:31). But this does not alter the New Testament's basic view of Satan as the incarnation of all evil power opposed to God; he is the enemy, and the breaking in of the kingdom of God depends upon his removal. When Satan in this duel is forced to capitulate, the New Testament is asserting that it is God who ultimately has the power.

A few more words are in order concerning the temptations of Jesus. The Synoptic Gospels all relate that Jesus was tempted by the devil, and contemporary research quite naturally has concluded that these accounts stem from traditions in the primitive church. In *The Testing of God's Son,* Gerhardsson shows that the long version of the temptation story (in Matthew and Luke) had Israel's *Shema* in mind.[4] When Jesus rejects the three temptations—to transform bread into stones, to throw himself down from the temple, to gain all the riches of the world by worshiping Satan—he thereby fulfills the threefold commandment to love God. Matthew wants to demonstrate that Jesus is perfect in his obedience to this law, in order subsequently to present him in the Sermon on the Mount as the messianic lawgiver.

To what extent was the kingdom of God to be observed and experienced during the earthly life of Jesus? This is a question closely related to what has just been said about the motif of struggle and the crisis situation. To begin with, let us take a look at one of the most contested and difficult texts on the kingdom of God: "The kingdom of God is not coming with signs to be observed; nor will they say, 'Lo, it is here!' or 'There!' for behold, the kingdom of God is in the midst of you" (Luke 17:20); the King James version has it "the kingdom of God is within you." The great majority of scholars hold that the former version is correct, the expression "within you" having no correspondence to other utterances of Jesus, and representing a spiritualism which is totally alien to him. There seems also to be general agreement that this word is no exception to the general rule that Jesus' words concerning the realization of the kingdom do not belong to the "present" but to the "coming era."[5] The context of this Lucan text points to the "coming"—but Luke, in accordance with his theology, counts on a longer course of historical time before the "end" is to arrive, a view which stands in contrast to the immediate expectations of apocalypticism.

There is widespread consensus that the debated words in Luke go back to an Aramaic saying of Jesus. What, then, do the words about the kingdom of God "in the midst of you" mean? Perrin, who has thoroughly discussed the text, summarizes his result in this way: the kingdom does not come in a way which can be observed by external indices; rather "we may claim that the meaning [of this passage] is: 'the Kingdom is a matter of human experience.' It does not come in such a way that it can be found by looking at the march of armies or the movement of heavenly bodies; it is not to be seen in the coming of messianic pretenders. Rather it is to be found wherever God is active decisively within the experience of an individual and men have faith to recognize this for what it is."[6] This possibility of discovery appears in the twin parables of the treasure in the field and the costly pearl (Matt. 13:44–46). Those who find and buy are in both cases putting all their eggs in one basket so as not to miss the unique opportunity which the nearness of the kingdom of God carries with it. God will come and reveal himself, making it evident that he has the power over the world and its kingdoms, over "death and all other powers of destruction." In contrast to the apocalyptics of his era, Jesus did not set an exact time for what was to take place. The important thing is to be prepared, although the "immediacy" of the kingdom determines the present and already invades the now. The power of demons is broken; it is a time of fulfillment, a time for a wedding feast, a time for joy. Jesus' expectations are certainly directed toward that which is to come: he expects the resurrection of the dead, judgment, and God's revealed dominion. But for Jesus there was no basic difference between the present and the future: "What mattered was to take seriously this nearness of God here and now. And the conversion that Jesus demanded meant precisely this."[7]

We have just touched on the question of Jesus' relation to apocalypticism. It now becomes necessary to take a close look at this complicated problem. For Schweitzer, Jesus was a "thoroughgoing apocalyptic," but that this was a highly one-sided view has slowly become clear. Certainly no one doubts that Jesus expected the "present era" to be followed in the near future by the "new era" of the kingdom of God—Jesus did not think in terms of a long historical perspective. Nonetheless, research has tended considerably to reduce the apocalyptic element in Jesus' proclamation. It does not now occur to anyone to describe Jesus' "ethic" as "interim ethic." Scholars have also pointed out that the apocalyptic texts in the gospels have in large measure been shaped by the primitive church, and it is extremely precarious to attempt to determine what might in this regard go back to Jesus himself. A summary of the views of certain scholars makes this point.

Braun's position has already been accounted for.[8] His *Jesus* does not contain any detailed analysis of relevant texts. The "apocalyptic" perspective is present, but "only the Father knows" when the end is to come. The primitive church enlarged on the apocalyptic theme, but, simultaneously, the motif was suppressed in the New Testament (in Luke and the later Pauline letters, and above all in the Gospel of John). Braun finds in this fact support for his thesis that the apocalyptic element in Jesus' proclamation was an error which must be disregarded.

Jeremias stresses the fact that there is no single saying of Jesus which postpones the expected transformation to a distant future. There can be no contesting the authenticity of a word such as this: "Truly I say to you, there are some standing here who will not taste death before they see that the kingdom of God has come with power" (Mark 9:1). On the other hand, there is no counterpart in Jesus to contemporary Jewish apocalyptic speculations concerning the sign and exact times. Jesus was interested in the fact that "God had granted a last period of grace" which had to be used. It is especially characteristic for Jesus, writes Jeremias in an extraordinary interpretation, that God, because of the prayers of those "who cry to him day and night" (Luke 18:7), can *"shorten* the time of distress—but God can also *lengthen* the period of grace" because of the prayer which asks that the unfruitful tree be allowed "to stand this year also" (Luke 13:6–9). These, says Jeremias, are among the most powerful words of Jesus: "Judgment is due, but God's will is not unalterable."[9]

Dodd quotes a few words from the important passage, Mark 13: "The sun will be darkened, the moon will not give her light, the stars will come falling from the sky, the celestial powers will be shaken. And then they will see the Son of man coming in the clouds with great power and glory" (vv. 24–26). Dodd says:

> Such images have a long history. They can be traced through many passages of poetry and prophesy in the Old Testament; they had a flourishing career in the "apocalypses" which pullulated in the period just before and just after the Christian era; and they lived on. It is impossible to say how far such passages as that quoted above are authentic utterances of Jesus, and how far the imagery has seeped into the gospel tradition from the environment. The images employed were part of the mental furniture of the period; there is no reason why Jesus should not have employed them. There is in any case nothing original about them. Where we may look for originality is the way they are applied, and the meaning attached to them. For while "apocalyptic" imagery was inherited, each writer was free to give his own interpretation, and nothing is clearer than that the interpretation varies from one to another.[10]

Were Jesus to have used such words as have been quoted above, "there is no reason to think that he had wanted to describe supernatural phenomena which in a literal sense could be 'seen.' " Jesus liked to use images in speaking, but it was not the apocalyptic imagery that was characteristic for him, but rather "the realism of the parables."

A major portion of Perrin's *Rediscovering the Teaching of Jesus* deals with "Jesus and the Future." In the parables of the sower, the mustard seed, and the leaven (Matt. 13 and parallels) he sees, as do so many other scholars (although Gerhardsson gives a totally different interpretation of these parables), the contrast between the humble beginning and the expected powerful results. These parables confirm Jesus' trust in "God's future"—God will legitimize Jesus' proclamation and ministry—and are intended to convey this trust to the listeners. The same aspect of "God's future" also meets us in the second petition of the Our Father and in the words "Many will come from east and west and sit at the table with Abraham, Isaac and Jacob" (Matt. 8:11). Table-fellowship within the community of Jesus is an anticipation of this future and its universal perspectives. Perrin also acknowledges that the word about the sign of Jonah, which is most difficult to interpret (Luke 11:30; Matt. 12:40) might be understood as referring to "some future event which will vindicate the message and ministry of Jesus, and be analogous to the deliverance of Jonah." Further, texts which deal with the realization of the kingdom of God before "this generation has perished" are not authentic words of Jesus; they all stem from the tradition of the primitive church.[11] Perrin asserts that this is also true of Mark 9:11, a passage whose authenticity, according to Jeremias, ought not to be questioned. The entire stress in Jesus' proclamation, according to Perrin, is that "the experience of the present is an anticipation of the future"—"the disciples' present has become God's present; God's future will be their future!"[12]

Our overview provides the following results. According to Braun, apocalyptic is richly represented in Jesus, but it can be written off as something conditioned by time and history. Jeremias warns against explaining away or belittling the apocalyptic element in Jesus. According to Dodd, apocalyptic is part and parcel of the mental furniture of the time and is not specific to Jesus. Perrin attempts to prove that in all essential matters the apocalyptic element in the gospels stems from the primitive church.

The Enigmatic Representative of the Kingdom of God

Thus far we have not dealt with the titles of high honor which are found in the gospels—chiefly "Messiah" and "Son of man." The question of Jesus' attitude to these titles has intentionally been reserved until this point in our study. This section has been given the rubric "The Enigmatic Representative of the Kingdom of God." The enigmatic element consists in the sovereignty with which the representative speaks and acts. The picture which scholarship has given in this regard stands in all essential matters as historically trustworthy—and this quite regardless of what may be concluded in respect to the christological titles.

The question of *whether* Jesus wanted to be the Messiah, and *in what sense* he might have wanted it, is a question which has been aired a great deal. During Jesus' lifetime the question of the Messiah was terribly important, and the Messiah then expected was a nationalistic one, who was to liberate and restore Israel and stand as a messianic king in the succession of David. Among Jesus' contemporaries such views were widespread and were most fanatically defended by the Zealots, in revolutionary opposition to the Roman occupation. It is obvious that Jesus' appearance and proclamation must have exercised a tremendous attraction and elicited expectations among those who adhered to the idea of a nationalistic Messiah; he was, writes Daniélou, "used" in their propaganda, and thus he aroused suspicion among the priestly hierarchy in Jerusalem.[13] Among the immediate circle of Jesus' disciples there was at least one—Simon—who was a Zealot; according to Oscar Cullmann,[14] it is possible that Peter was also, and probable that Judas Iscariot was. This nationalistic messianism followed Jesus like a shadow during all of his ministry, even up to Pilate's death sentence and the inscription on the cross. Was it more than an awkward companion? Was it, as the temptation stories hint, a temptation which Jesus fought? Were there, to go a step further, any traits in his behavior which coincided with the political ambitions of the Zealots? The question is ancient; it dates back even to the Enlightenment and H. S. Reimarus, who is usually called the father of historical-critical Jesus research. It has never since ceased to be posed, and within the last ten years it has again come to the fore through studies which present Jesus as a political revolutionary.[15] The mainstream of scholarship, however, has followed and still follows another train of thought:

107

it has always claimed that Jesus, whether he wanted to be the Messiah or not, shaped his message in direct opposition to messianic nationalism. The fact that the gospels contain traits that *may* be interpreted in revolutionary and nationalistic ways does not—it is said—weigh heavily in comparison with the overwhelming evidence that his intention was totally other.

Jesus never called himself the Messiah—the two passages in the texts in which the term is found (Mark 9:41; Matt. 23:10) are generally understood as secondary additions. According to the majority of scholars, he did not even want the title "Son of David." We shall now listen to two quite different, yet each in its own way representative, interpretations of Jesus' relation to the messianic question: one by Dodd, and the other by Ferdinand Hahn, who has devoted a thick volume, *The Titles of Jesus in Christology*, to the titles of honor.[16]

Dodd treats the messianic problem with great care. After having determined that Jesus never spontaneously made any claim to be the Messiah, he examines the context of two texts in which the question can be discussed. The first time this happens is when Peter at Caesarea Philippi confesses: "You are the Messiah." According to Mark and Luke, Jesus' only reaction is a sharp admonition to the disciples that they must not say anything about this to anyone. The *most* we can say about this, writes Dodd, is that "Jesus did not refuse the title." Matthew has a different view. He has, like the other evangelists, recorded the command against speaking about the matter; but in contrast to the others, he lets Jesus accept the title and praise Peter. The second time the messianic question crops up is when the high priest examines Jesus and asks the question point-blank: "Are you the Messiah?" According to Mark, Jesus gives an affirmative answer, whereas in Matthew and Luke his answer is evasive. The same evasiveness reoccurs when the accusation against Jesus has been duly adjusted to Roman ears, and Pilate asks if he is the King of the Jews. Dodd paraphrases Jesus' answer, "You say so," with the words, "Have it so if you choose . . . At this juncture a refusal to disown the title would have the same effect as an avowal, and it was a matter of life and death. Jesus at any rate allowed himself to be condemned to death for claiming to be (in Jewish terms) Messiah."[17]

When Dodd subsequently attempts to determine what messiahship might have meant to Jesus, he refers to the main theme in his book, programmatically titled *The Founder of Christianity*.

> Jesus set himself to constitute the new Israel under his own leadership; he nominated its foundation members, and admitted them into the new "covenant," and laid down its new law. That was his mission. If it did not entirely agree with any of the contemporary ideas of what the Messiah should do, there was no other term available which came near to covering it. He could not deny his mission; he could not disavow the authority that went with it; and therefore, if the question was posed, he could not simply repudiate the title "Messiah." But it was an embarrassment to him, and he preferred that it should not be used publicly, until at last his hand was forced. In the popular mind messiahship was associated with the political and military role of the "Son of David." To play that part was the last thing Jesus desired. Any suggestion that he proposed to do so was a hindrance to his true work and a danger to his cause. His appeal to his people must rest on something other than a debatable claim to messiahship.[18]

The sharp words which Jesus directs at Peter ("Get away with you, Tempter," as transcribed by Dodd) when Peter wants to prevent him from following the road to suffering and death, confirm what a chasm there was between Jesus' idea of the Messiah and that of traditional nationalism.

When Dodd subsequently introduces the passage from Isaiah concerning the Servant of the Lord, it is important that he takes the primitive church as his point of departure. When that church stood before the suffering and death of its founder, it found an explanation in the text on the suffering Servant of the Lord. Matthew introduces in one passage a four-verse-long quotation from one of Isaiah's texts, beginning with the words: "Behold, my servant whom I have chosen, my beloved with whom my soul is well pleased. I will put my spirit upon him" (Matt. 12:18). We have, says Dodd, "good reason to think that Jesus himself first directed the attention of his followers to the figure of the Servant. He did so because by reflecting on it they might be led to a juster idea of what it was to be 'Messiah.' 'You think as men think, not as God thinks,' he said to Peter; we might venture to paraphrase: 'Your Messiah is a conqueror; God's Messiah is a servant.' "[19]

Dodd points out that there is a fusion of the two ideal figures of Messiah in the account of Jesus' baptism, where the Spirit, like a dove, descends on him and the voice from heaven says: "You are my Son, my Beloved; on you my favor rests." Should we want to interpret the symbolism, we will find that the words of the voice come from the Old Testament. The words "You are my Son" were directed to the King of Israel, prototype of the Messiah. "My Beloved, on you my favor rests" refers to the Servant of the Lord in Isaiah. This Servant was prepared for his task by the gift of the Spirit. In this way the gospels have given us a symbolic shorthand sketch of Jesus' task and equipment as the Messiah.

Ferdinand Hahn begins his presentation of "the significance of the Messiah concept in the life of Jesus" with an investigation of Jesus' relation to the Zealots and to the national ideal of the Messiah. He rejects the notion of any connection between Jesus and the Zealots. For example, the fact that Jesus had disciples who came from this section of the population does not prove anything; his disciples came from every possible background, one being a publican. The statement that Jesus did not come to bring peace but a sword (Matt. 10:34) means not that he wanted to put weapons into the hands of his disciples; it implies that the anxiety and struggle of the end-time had begun. The admonition to sell the mantle and buy a sword (Luke 22:36) must be regarded as figurative speech; the point is that a new situation had been introduced in which life itself was at stake.[20]

If Zealot traits, however, were absent in Jesus, one cannot therefore conclude that he was altogether unacquainted with the general messianic ideal. The texts on the entry into Jerusalem and the cleansing of the temple seem to indicate the opposite. If one claims that the nationalistic Messiah was an idea alien to Jesus, one must not put too much stock in his riding an ass and thereby seemingly identifying himself with the humble rider of Zechariah 9:9. The accounts of the entry are ambiguous, and they have evidently been enlarged upon in the primitive church. It appears accurate that Jesus was in fact greeted by Passover pilgrims with the cry: "Blessed be he who comes in the name of the Lord" (Psalm 118:25). Had it been a question of an authentic messianic demonstration, the Romans would undoubtedly have interfered immediately, and Pilate would not even have hesitated to pronounce the death sentence. But *if* the entry was not a messianic demonstration, neither was the so-called cleansing of the temple. It was in reality no "cleansing of the temple." Jesus' act was undertaken in the "courtyard of the Gentiles" and it can best be interpreted as a "parabolic act."

In an investigation of the difficult Marcan narrative of Peter's messianic confession, Hahn points out that the text in its present "Christianized" form shows itself to have been composed by Mark. Jesus' harsh words to Peter must be considered original—they could not have originated after Easter. According to Hahn, Jesus not only rejected the Jewish ideal of the Messiah but also the title itself. The title was subsequently developed in the primitive church in such a way as to make its use in respect to the earthly Jesus possible.

The text on the trial before the Sanhedrin does not give any trustworthy historical information concerning either the accusations or Jesus' answer. It is not at all certain that a death sentence was pronounced. It is "not unlikely" that the session was merely informative in character and that its intention was to prepare for the accusations before Pilate. Hahn's conclusion is that Jesus totally rejected the picture of the messianic king and that he "most probably" refused the title of the Messiah, although he was accused and sentenced as a messianic rebel. Within the primitive church the idea of the Messiah developed at different, subsequent stages. At first, when the inscription on the cross was still fresh in mind, one did not speak easily about the Messiah. But soon enough the thought of Jesus as a royal Messiah surfaced again. It was injected into an apocalyptic context and was attached to the expected *parousia*: the final act of Jesus as messianic king would be accomplished at the end of time. When the *parousia* did not come, the title took on even greater significance. The Messiah who was to return was already reigning all over the world; the Messiah who had previously been seen as "the Son of man" now became closely identified with Jesus, the Lord—*Kyrios*. At the next level the Messiah-Christ became integral to the Passion story: the idea of the suffering Messiah developed and was confirmed with proof from Scripture. At the very last stage messiahship was to concern all of Jesus' earthly ministry, and "Christ" became a proper name.

If interpretations of the question of the Messiah vary, those concerning the "Son of man" vary even more. Common to many views, however, is the fact that—in Bultmann's tradition—three different categories of words concerning the Son of man are identified: those which refer to the coming Son of man and thus have apocalyptic traits; those which appear in the present tense and deal with the life of Jesus (they usually replace the first person pronoun); and finally, those which are connected with sayings about immediate suffering and death. There is ample space for a number of different theories here: are all three categories authentic? Does one or another category have a reliable background? Do none? Material which provides the historical background of the term "Son of man" can be cited briefly. Two Old Testament passages function as a solid foundation. The first can be found in the book on Daniel: "I saw in the night visions, and behold, with the clouds of heaven there came one like a son of man, and he came to the Ancient of Days and was presented before him" (7:13). The second one is from the book of Psalms: "The Lord says to my lord: 'Sit at my right hand, till I make your enemies my footstool'" (Psalm 110:1). The title also occurs several times in intertestamental apocalyptic literature. Any scholar's evaluation of this literature and its importance influences the view which is offered of the Son of man in the New Testament.

Let us first of all listen to Hahn, who has devoted such attention to the titles of high honor. Within critical research there is, says Hahn, a certain consensus concerning the sayings about suffering: that in their present form, at any rate, they stem from the tradition of the primitive community. There are different opinions as to which of the two other categories is primary: the eschatological words about the Son of man, or those which deal with the life of the earthly Jesus. Hahn, however, claims that the eschatological Son of man represents the oldest level. It was in this sense that Jesus spoke of the Son of man when, for example, it is written: "And I tell you, every one who acknowledges me before men, the Son of man also will acknowledge before the angels of God; but he who denies me before men will be denied before the angels of God" (Luke 12:8–9). The parallel text in Mark is both later and an expansion. It is quite apparent, according to Hahn, that the Son of man of whom Jesus speaks here is someone other than himself.

It was after Easter that the earthly Jesus was identified with the Son of man. This happened rapidly, and the picture of the "coming Jesus–Son of man" which emerged was then shaped with the traditional apocalyptical elements. It is easy to understand this identification, since Jesus, in such passages as the one just quoted, had asserted that the coming Son of man would give credence to what had happened in the life of the earthly Jesus. "The Son of man" now became a christological title for the earthly Jesus. Latest of all to develop was the group of "Son of man" sayings in which that title became attached to words about Jesus' suffering and resurrection. There are different layers of these, the very latest being texts which refer to proof in Scripture (for example, Mark 14:21). On the whole, this latter group of sayings attests to the power of the christological conception within the primitive church.[21]

In this connection we must refer to Geza Vermes, a Jewish scholar who has devoted considerable attention to Jesus. He is one of the many Jewish scholars who in recent years have made basic and positive contributions to Jesus research. The main part of his book is devoted to examining the earlier Jewish and intertestamental background of the christological titles which the New Testament applies to Jesus. He concludes that Jesus never wanted to be called the Messiah; that title referred to a king in the line of David, the conqueror of the heathen, the savior and restorer of Israel—all of which was alien to Jesus. But from the point of view of the temple hierarchy and the Roman occupation forces in Jerusalem, Galilee was regarded with great suspicion: it was both the point of origin and the refuge of the rebels. A Galilean who gathered crowds of people around himself was by that very fact highly suspect, and it was self-evident that Jesus would be the object of such suspicion. In reality the national messianic ideal followed him incessantly, even to the inscription on the cross.[22] Concerning the phrase "Son of man," Vermes claims that in the Jewish intertestamental literature it was never used as a title with definite content, but consistently had a neutral force: the word means "I" or "man." For this reason alone it is clear to Vermes that Jesus the Galilean did not use "Son of man" as a title of honor.

If Jesus, as Hahn and Vermes believe, never spoke about himself as the Son of man, Jeremias differs in claiming that he actually did so in a limited number of instances. In the Synoptics the title occurs—disregarding parallel passages—thirty-eight times. At certain points the word only meant "the man" or "man"; in many cases the word is missing in a "competing tradition" and must then be taken to mean simply "I." The result of this investigation leads Jeremias to conclude that the word was used as a title only ten times, and then with reference to a coming Son of man. Are there any authentic words of Jesus here? Jeremias isolates five occasions on which Jesus spoke of the Son of man in the third person, something which can hardly date back to the primitive church. It is especially important that nowhere in these texts is anything said about the resurrection or the *parousia*. Jeremias finds Dodd convincing in his proof that Jesus did not differentiate between the resurrection, the *parousia*, the fulfillment, and the new temple; all these expressions confirmed one and the same thing: God's victory. This underscores the view that we are dealing here with sayings which were in existence before Easter, and the conclusion follows that the oldest usage of "Son of man" words originated with Jesus himself.[23]

In intertestamental apocalyptic Jeremias holds that there are two different conceptions of the Messiah–Son of man: one is the traditional Jewish notion, and the other still preserves traits of nationalistic messianism inasmuch as it conceives of him as conquering the heathen rulers. But in this second conception he is also a superhuman figure with transcendent qualities and a universal significance, "a light of the nations."[24] Jesus' words about the Son of man relate to this picture without the nationalistic elements. "Son of man" is a title of honor, a *terminus gloriae*. He will appear suddenly as lightning from a clear sky (Matt. 24:37, 39). He will fulfill the prophesy of Daniel and will be "coming in clouds with great power and glory" (Mark 13:26). The Son of man in Daniel was thought to come from below and upwards, but in the gospels he is thought to come from above and downwards.[25] The fact that Jesus speaks of the Son of man in the third person singular does not mean that he is referring to anyone other than himself. It is inconceivable that Jesus should have thought of himself as a "precursor" of another, in the fashion of John the Baptist. When Jesus speaks of himself in the third person, he speaks of himself as exalted. How would Jesus, asks Jeremias, cope with the contrast of his present powerlessness to his future glory? The answer is that we shall evidently not get at the heart of Jesus' awareness of his mission by referring to Daniel's Son of man—that awareness is more deeply anchored in Isaiah's Servant of the Lord.

In contrast to Jeremias, Norman Perrin finds the intertestamental apocalyptic literature to be so rich in variations that it is not possible to distill from it a picture of a specific Son of man which might stand as an alternative to the Messiah of the Jewish tradition.[26] Thereby the importance of this literature for Jesus is considerably reduced. Actually, Jesus did not identify himself with any apocalyptic Son of man. Perrin divides the texts which claim authenticity into three categories: those which refer to Daniel, sayings of judgment, and "comparison sayings." To the first category belong sayings about the Son of man coming "in clouds with great power and glory" (Mark 13:26, 14:62). These texts, like others in the New Testament, presuppose that the resurrection is primarily an ascension, a conception which relies on the Son of man in Daniel—where the travel is upward from below—and on the words in Psalm 110 concerning his place at the right hand of God. The words reflect an early Christian exegetical tradition and are not based on Jesus' proclamation. Representative of the words of judgment, according to Perrin, are the sayings that the acknowledgement and denial of Jesus will be verified by the Son of man before God's angels. The "Son of man" comes from the tradition, but Perrin counts with the possibility that an original form could date back to Jesus, perhaps this one: "Everyone who acknowledges me before men, the Son of man also will acknowledge before the angels of God" (Luke 12:8). In the "comparison" group Perrin cites, among others, the saying about the sign of Jonah, the assertion that the men of Nineveh and the queen of the South will join in the judgment upon "this generation" (Luke 11:31). Both Matthew's interpretation of the sign of Jonah as referring to Jesus' death and resurrection, and Luke's interpretation, which refers to the coming Son of man as judge, stem, as does the word "Son of man," from the primitive church. Perrin's conclusion is that Jesus could not have spoken of a coming apocalyptic Son of man, either in reference to himself or to another eschatological figure. If Jesus referred at all to Daniel's imagery, it was to assert the certainty of a future "vindication," a sanction of his own activity and of man's response. The same certainty is also expressed in the words about the sign of Jonah and in the words about Nineveh's men and the queen of the South. We are dealing throughout with a question of legitimization of what is to come, but nothing is said about the form of that future, except that it lies ahead.

If the three scholars we have cited have expressed themselves concerning the Son of man with striking conciseness, albeit in different ways, Dodd is much more cautious. The term is, he says, as unnatural in Greek as it is common in Aramaic, where the word quite simply means "man" or "the man." Such is the case with the sayings attributed to Jesus: "Son of man" is then synonymous with "I." In other cases, where Jesus seems to refer to someone other than himself, it may be that he has chosen to speak "in an indirect form of language" in order to stress his own special role, his vocation. It is striking that the term occurs so often in connection with the suffering and death that lie before him, as well as in connection with the forthcoming "resurrection" and "return." It is "perhaps impossible" to determine what Jesus actually said, but "the idea of new life through death, of victory coming out of defeat, is an inseparable part of the thought of Jesus about his destiny."[27]

In connection with sayings such as "They will see the Son of man coming in the clouds," there are, however, a great many problems:

> Of course it is imaginative symbolism; but what does it symbolize? We cannot but recognize here traits of the "apocalyptic" hopes and speculations which, with a long ancestry behind them, revived in strength during the feverish years that preceded the fall of Jerusalem. We can understand that they seized avidly upon any remembered words of their Lord which seemed to have a bearing upon them. Should we be right in suspecting that his reporters, understandably anxious to find his words relevant to their own urgent preoccupations, have given them a twist away from their original intentions? There is reason to believe they have sometimes done so.
>
> Yet we should here proceed with caution. It is reasonable to suppose that Jesus himself would have employed the imagery which was traditional and familiar among his contemporaries. If Jesus did use it, it does not follow, either that he intended it to be taken literally, or that he meant by it just what his reporters supposed.[28]

Here, writes Dodd, we must start from the standpoint of sayings which are central to Jesus' proclamation: the kingdom of God is here. This kingdom can be experienced in the present and can be discovered by those who see:

> But at the same time there is more than meets the eye. It is the *reign* of God; it is the eternal God himself, here present. There is a power at work in this world which is not of this world, something "super-natural," an invasion from the Beyond—however you choose to express it. It gives an eternal dimension to the temporal present, and to each succeeding "present"; but it can never be exhausted in any temporal present, however deeply significant. The kingdom of God, while it is present experience, remains also a hope, but a hope directed to a consummation beyond history.

116

To express this aspect of the kingdom Jesus was content to make use of long-established symbols—a feast with the blessed dead who are "alive to God," a great assize with "all nations" standing at the bar. These are not forthcoming events, to which the spirit of man awakes when it is done with the past, present and future. This is the kingdom of God in the fullness of its meaning, and it lies beyond history. And yet it "came" in history, in that crucial episode of which Jesus was himself the active center.

The last judgment is "essentially" a judgment which men pass on themselves by their different answers to Jesus; thus it is a judgment within the framework of history. "But its significance is expressed in the dramatic picture of all nations gathered before the throne of the heavenly Judge."[29]

It is in this light that we may best understand "the cryptic words" about the coming Son of man, using as background the passages from Daniel and Psalm 110. It is a vision of God's victory over all the powers of the universe, the consummation of the kingdom of God "beyond history." But "this victory has its embodiment in history, namely in the impending fate of Jesus himself, who is to pass through suffering and sacrifice to glorious life. The human figure of Daniel's vision has acquired a new identity. It is the historical Person in whom, as its 'inclusive representative,' the new Israel, the people of God, is to emerge. His ultimate 'coming' lies beyond history."[30]

To this section on the christological titles in the Synoptic Gospels we must finally add a few words concerning the expression "the Son," which Jesus, according to two texts, is held to have used about himself. One is from Mark: "But of that day or that hour no one knows, not even the angels in heaven, nor the Son, but only the Father" (13:32). It is generally agreed that this saying stems from Jesus, although this could hardly be true of the term "the Son"—even Jeremias, who in many cases is prone to advocate authenticity, considers "nor the Son" a later explanatory addition.[31] The meaning, however, remains the same even when the two words are deleted.

The second text is in Matthew (11:25–27; Luke 10:21–22): "I thank thee, Father, Lord of heaven and earth, that thou hast hidden these things from the wise and understanding and revealed them to the babes; yea, Father, for such was thy gracious will. All things have been delivered to me by my Father; and no one knows the Son except the Father, and no one knows the Father except the Son and any one

117

to whom the Son chooses to reveal him." Braun and others think that there is a basis for authenticity for the first part of this passage. Concerning the words about the Father and the Son, Braun is of the opinion that they have no authenticity because of the "Hellenistic-Oriental" character of the language. Hahn and Jeremias, in contrast, agree that the language is characteristically Semitic. According to Hahn, however, the "absolute" words about the Father and the Son, as well as the expression *"my* Father," can hardly be authentic—they have been formed against the background of Jesus' use of *abba* in addressing God, and stem from the primitive church. Jeremias, on the contrary, claims authenticity for these words on the grounds that they are a central saying of Jesus concerning his mission. It is not totally unique; an analogous consciousness of mission can be found—although different in all other respects—in the "teacher of righteousness" in Qumran. That which Jesus says here resonates in different ways in the texts; he reveals to the disciples the mystery (*mysterion*) of the kingdom of God (Mark 4:11); his activity reflects God's attitude to sinners (Luke 15). Jesus' consciousness of his mission is intimately bound with his *abba* to God. Jeremias rejects the long-standing idea that we are here dealing with a "Johannine" addition. This is, rather, a theme which John expanded on later.[32]

According to Dodd, this joyful cry of Jesus and his words about the inner relation between the Father and the Son are to be understood in contrast to a pervasive lack of understanding of him and his message. Jesus' spontaneous cry shows that his heart, in the midst of the storms around him, possessed "a center of calm": ". . . there is One who does know him—God, his Father. And in that same, intimate, personal way he too knows God. Here, we may legitimately infer, is to be found the driving force and the source of energy for an almost impossible mission . . ."[33]

The overview which we have now presented of the views of different scholars in regard to the christological titles has shown that we are moving on uncertain ground. Whether we should be content with merely stating differences of opinion is another question. There is actually fairly wide agreement in regard to Jesus' attitude—that is, to Jesus as the enigmatic representative of the kingdom of God. Whatever may be the case with the titles, it remains clear that Jesus acted with total sovereignty on behalf of God, enigmatically sovereign in both word and deed.   And compared to this fact, the question of the titles seems secondary.   In a work entitled *The Continuing Search for the Historical Jesus,* the Norwegian scholar Jacob Jervell writes: "We said that it was doubtful that Jesus used the messianic titles of himself. From this we might easily draw the wrong conclusion, the conclusion that Jesus represented himself as something less than the Messiah, a very ordinary person.   The sources give us no basis for such a conclusion.   On the contrary, the fact is that Jesus claimed to be something more than the Messiah, something that could not be expressed by this title."[34]   There is profound truth to this statement.

Notes

1. Birger Gerhardsson, "Bibelns ethos," *Etik och kristen tro,* ed. Gustaf Wingren (Lund: Gleerups, 1971), p. 33.

2. Cf. pp. 55ff. above.

3. Joachim Jeremias, *New Testament Theology,* trans. John Bowden (New York: Scribner's, and London: SCM, 1971), p. 95.

4. Birger Gerhardsson, *The Testing of God's Son,* trans. John Toy (Lund: Gleerups, 1966).

5. Bent Noack, *Guds Rige i os eller iblandt os* (Copenhagen: G. E. C. Gads, 1967), pp. 57–70, 86–90.

6. Norman Perrin, *Rediscovering the Teaching of Jesus* (New York: Harper & Row, and London: SCM, 1967), p. 74.

7. Eta Linnemann, *Jesus of the Parables,* trans. John Sturdy (New York: Harper & Row, and London: S.P.C.K., 1964), p. 102.

8. Cf. pp. 18ff. above.

9. Jeremias, *New Testament Theology,* p. 139–40.

10. C. H. Dodd, *The Founder of Christianity* (New York: Macmillan, and London: Collier-Macmillan, 1970), pp. 42–43.

11. Perrin, *Rediscovering the Teaching of Jesus,* p. 194.

12. Ibid., p. 204.

13. Jean Daniélou, "Un mouvement juif parmi d'autres" in the collection *Jésus,* p. 99.

14. Oscar Cullman, *Jesus and the Revolutionaries,* trans. Gareth Putnam (New York: Harper & Row, 1970), p. 9.

15. For a comprehensive survey of this question, including extensive bibliographical information, cf. Martin Hengel, *Victory Over Violence: Jesus and the Revolutionists,* trans. David E. Green with an introduction by Robin Scroggs (Philadelphia: Fortress, and London: S.P.C.K., 1973).

16. Ferdinand Hahn, *The Titles of Jesus in Christology: Their History in*

Early Christianity, trans. Harold Knight and George Ogg (Cleveland: World, and London: Lutterworth, 1969).

17. Dodd, *The Founder of Christianity,* p. 102.

18. Ibid., pp. 102–03.

19. Ibid., p. 105.

20. Hahn, *The Titles of Jesus in Christology,* pp. 154–55.

21. Ibid., pp. 21–53.

22. Geza Vermes, *Jesus the Jew: A Historian's Reading of the Gospels* (London: Collins, 1973), pp. 145–56, 160–86.

23. Jeremias, *New Testament Theology,* pp. 272ff., 308–11.

24. Ibid., p. 275.

25. Ibid., p. 273.

26. Perrin, *Rediscovering the Teaching of Jesus,* pp. 164–99; for further developments in Perrin's thought see his two works *A Modern Pilgrimage in New Testament Christology* (Philadelphia: Fortress, 1974) and *Jesus and the Language of the Kingdom* (Philadelphia: Fortress, 1976).

27. Dodd, *The Founder of Christianity,* p. 113.

28. Ibid., pp. 114–15.

29. Ibid., pp. 115–16.

30. Ibid., pp. 117–18.

31. Jeremias, *New Testament Theology,* p. 238.

32. Ibid., pp. 56–61.

33. Dodd, *The Founder of Christianity,* p. 52.

34. Jacob Jervell, *The Continuing Search for the Historical Jesus,* trans. Harris E. Kaasa (Minneapolis: Augsburg, 1965), p. 47.

6

THE EARTHLY JESUS AND FAITH IN CHRIST IN THE PRIMITIVE CHURCH

Resurrection Faith

If we were strictly to adhere to the subject matter of this book—the earthly Jesus—our report would now be complete. But this would be to stop at the point where the question marks are the most frequent. What do scholars have to say about the Easter accounts of the gospels? Most of the works we have considered have nothing at all to say, for the simple reason that the theme has not been a part of the more or less limited area of study with which they have dealt. There are three, however—Braun, Dodd, and Jeremias—who have attempted to render accounts in full.

Braun's exposition is brief. He says, as we have already seen, that Jesus' authority was transformed; whereas during his life on earth his authority was immediate and unmotivated, in the primitive church it came to be associated with christological titles referring in part to his continued existence after death, and in part to his heavenly pre-existence, existence in the form of God (Phil. 2:6). The decisive factor in this development was the conviction of his followers that the crucified one "did not remain in death." An old tradition of Jewish-Christian origin speaks of visions in which the resurrected one appeared to his followers (1 Cor. 15:5-8), to individuals (Peter, Jacob, and Paul), and also to groups of people. Such visions must have extended over several years, for when Paul's vision took place there was already a congregation in Damascus. He can describe the heavenly vision succinctly: "God was pleased to reveal his Son to me" (Gal. 1:16). This tradition of visions was combined with traditions of Jesus' resurrection—and there seems also to have been an old tradition of the immediate elevation of the crucified one (Phil. 2:9; Hebrews 1:3).

In the Gospel of Luke the ascension takes place on the same day as the resurrection, whereas in Acts it takes place after forty days. According to Braun, it is possible, however, that the latter text is not original. Not until the tradition was in the process of expansion did the "empty tomb" have any significance for the message of the resurrection. All three Synoptics report the empty tomb, even though their information may be somewhat contradictory.

We can hardly identify with the by no means unambiguous world view or conceptual framework of the first Christians. This matter is even less clear when we remember that in antiquity, similar phenomena were attributed to nature gods, heroes, great philosophers, and important rulers. "Faith in the resurrection is an ancient Christian . . . expression for the authority which Jesus had won. . . . This expression cannot have binding power today. But the authority Jesus intended may well be binding for us."[1]

Dodd's analysis is more deliberate. The question at issue is how Jesus' followers became convinced that he was alive. John is the only one who mentions that the empty tomb had significance for belief in the resurrection; the two disciples who ran to the grave "saw and believed." Has he, asks Dodd, written this in order to prepare for the climax of what he has to say about seeing and believing: "Blessed are those who have not seen and yet believe" (John 20:29)? "It may be so." In no other case has an evangelist spoken of the empty tomb as a cause of faith. Rather, the stress is upon encounters with the resurrected Lord. The evangelists—"perhaps through experiences which had been made in attempts at creating trust in the message"—were conscious of the fact that the empty tomb could not verify the resurrection—"the body could have been carried away by friendly or unfriendly hands." In other parts of the New Testament the resurrection is a central theme, but the empty tomb is not mentioned. When, in writings older than the gospels, it is said that "Christ had risen from the dead" or that "he was buried and had risen on the third day," the thought of some kind of reawakening of the body was readily available to the Jewish Christians, who already believed in the resurrection of the dead. "Is it possible, then," asks Dodd, "that the earliest Christians, convinced on other grounds that Jesus was still alive, gave expression to this conviction in an imaginative or symbolic form suggested by the common belief, and that this was the origin of the story in the gospels?" Dodd answers, "It may be so. Or, again, it may not."[2] He proposes the following possibility: tradition has preserved a genuine memory of the empty tomb on Sunday morning; at first it seemed confusing and perplexing, but it was later understood that Jesus in some way had left the tomb. The question cannot be answered by the historian.

At any rate, the stress is on the fact that Jesus, after his death, was "seen" alive. Dodd scrutinizes the texts beginning with the oldest testimony in Paul (1 Cor. 15). If taken literally, the accounts of these encounters with the risen Lord are problematic and even contradictory—that which is described lies on the borderline of or beyond normal human behavior. Attempts are sometimes made at defending and even rationalizing that which, to the original witnesses, was "an immediate, intuitive certainty which did not need any justification." They were "dead sure" that they had met Jesus, and that was that. Their personal relationship had been re-established, they had been restored after the fiasco in the hour of their trial. They were new men in a new world, trusting and courageous, prepared to assume leadership of a movement which had quickly assumed astonishing strength.

Something had happened to these people. They claimed to have met Jesus. We cannot prove the contrary. We can know nothing of the character of these encounters, but we can know ever so much more about their results: they were the creative beginning of a new series of events. They gave rise to the birth of a new fellowship—or, as they would have put it themselves, to a "rebirth of God's people."

Jeremias, like Braun, believes that the "Christophanies" lasted for several years and that tradition of a much later date limited them to forty days. Jeremias records a number of secondary traits in the resurrection accounts. First of all, there was in the oldest tradition a deep need to attach the Christophanies to words which were spoken by the risen one: most primitively, a hailing by name or a greeting of peace; at a later stage, longer speeches and dialogues. Another secondary trait is of apologetic nature. Against the charge that the disciples stole Jesus' body during the night stands the legend of the Roman centurion at the tomb. The allegation that the resurrection was a series of hallucinations is similarly put to rest by the claim that Jesus had shown his hands and feet, had had his body touched, and had eaten a meal of fried fish in the presence of his disciples. Secondary trait is of an apologetic nature. Against the charge that the baptismal formula (Matt. 28:19) and directives concerning mission.[3]

In contrast, the oldest layer of tradition is characterized by over-powering and enigmatic phenomena: opened eyes at the breaking of bread, heavenly radiance, and the unexpected appearance in closed rooms followed by sudden disappearance. The reactions on the part of the witnesses are intimately connected with all this: they have difficulty recognizing the risen one; they are blinded by heavenly radiance; they think that they are seeing a ghost. Fright and anxiety, uncertainty and doubt are mingled with joy and adoration. In Matthew: "And when they saw him they worshiped him: but some doubted" (28:17). In Luke: "They (simply) could not believe (it) for joy" (24:41; Jeremias' translation).

A few matters characteristic of Jeremias' approach to the text need mentioning.[4] Mark 16:1–8 is a secondary and late passage which attempts to prove the resurrection by means of the empty tomb—it is regrettable that scholars for so long have viewed this passage as the *Urtext*. The oldest text can be found in the latest—in terms of literary genre—Gospel, John, in which Mary Magdalene comes alone to the tomb. On discovering that the tomb has been opened, she hurries to tell Peter. On her return to the tomb, she first of all experiences a vision of an angel, and then a Christophany, but nobody is about to believe what she has to tell them. Then follows Peter's Christophany, which totally changes the picture and releases "an avalanche" of Christophanies. This is documented both by Paul (1 Cor. 15:5) and by Luke: "The Lord has risen indeed, and has appeared to Simon!" (24:34). Jeremias finds it remarkable that in spite of "the fundamental significance of this appearance of Christ to Peter it is never portrayed as the first appearance"; indeed, Matthew not only keeps silent about the matter but even omits the words of greeting "especially to Peter" which appear in Mark. The reason for this intentional pushing aside of Peter is, according to Jeremias, the fact that extreme Jewish Christians were offended by Peter's positive attitude toward uncircumcised Gentiles (Gal. 2:12b; Acts 11:2).

The disciples experienced the events of Easter as God's new creation, the breakthrough of a new era. A peculiar and yet tangible witness to the atmosphere in that early time is the passage in Matthew which records what happened in the hour of Jesus' death: "And behold, the curtain of the temple was torn in two, from top to bottom; and the earth shook, and the rocks split, the tombs were also opened, and many bodies of the saints who had fallen asleep were raised, and coming out of the tombs after his resurrection they went into the holy city and appeared to many" (27:51–53). That this is a very old text can be proven by the inserted words "after his resurrection," which attempt to confirm that Jesus as the risen one was, as Paul says, "the first fruits of those who had fallen asleep" (1 Cor. 15:20).

One reflection of the Easter experience is the notion that Jesus' resurrection meant his immediate ascension to the throne: he took the place to the right of God, inheriting the kingdom. When this access to power did not immediately or visibly manifest itself, the ascension was subsequently viewed as an act preliminary to a final and definitive one. This distinction was one of sheer necessity and is full of contradictions, confirming that the original reaction on the part of the disciples was different. These words in Matthew support this: "To me is given all power in heaven and on earth" (28:18). The disciples experienced Easter as "the beginning of the last days." They saw Jesus in radiance. They were witnesses to his access to power. This means *they experienced the parousia.*

It may be of interest to compare Jeremias' approach to the Christophanies with that of the French philosopher of religion, Marcel Légaut. In his interesting book *Introduction à l'intelligence du passé et de l'avenir du christianisme* (1971), he describes these revelations as charismatic phenomena. The presupposition for the disciples' ability to take part in these phenomena was their faith in Jesus, which had originated during his life on earth. It was not a miracle to be shared by everyone. Charismatic phenomena appear to those who are inwardly prepared (*interieurment préparés*) and who need them in order to be faithful to their mission. These extraordinary phenomena are not the cause of the disciples' faith, but they are given to them "in a situation which from a human point of view was impossible to bear without extraordinary help." This help confirms their faith (Paul would certainly not embrace this kind of argument). Légaut calls the Christophanies charismatic[5]—Jeremias appears to agree when he calls them pneumatic. *"The appearance of Christ to Paul* which is mentioned last in 1 Cor. 15:3ff., and which consisted in a vision of shining light . . . clearly attests the pneumatic character of the Christophanies . . .; it may be regarded as typical of all of them."[6]

The three scholars we have considered all dealt with the question of the resurrection as a sort of postscript, and therefore only briefly addressed themselves to the problem. We shall, then, take a look at a more detailed study by Ulrich Wilckens: *Auferstehung. Das biblische Auferstehungszeugnis historisch undersucht und erklärt.*[7] One of the merits of this book is that, as background, it has examined what the Old Testament and the intertestamental literature say about the resurrection.

The earliest New Testament text on the resurrection is found in Paul (1 Cor. 15). A number of persons to whom Jesus "appeared" are enumerated in this passage: first of all, Peter (Cephas), who, according to Wilckens, occupies a fully identified position. Nor is there reason to question the name of James. Quite a few scholars, however, doubt that visions appeared to a large number of people: "Actually one cannot, without difficulty, imagine a vision in front of a group of persons," writes Wilckens.[8] In his vision Paul experiences Jesus as the exalted one, the "heavenly" one, and Peter seems to have experienced him in a similar way. The oldest tradition does not know of an "ascension"; resurrection was in itself exaltation. Paul conceives of Jesus' resurrection as a mighty act of God "who gives life to the dead" (Rom. 4:17). To him it was especially important that Christ was raised "as the first fruit of those who had fallen asleep" (1 Cor. 15:20).

Mark 16:1–8 is, according to Wilckens, a body of tradition from the first congregation in Jerusalem which has been added to the Passion story as a conclusion: by men crucified, by God exalted—he "is not here," he is with God. Matthew's account has its high point in Galilee, where the disciples are solemnly given authority to work as his apostles. To Matthew, furthermore, resurrection equaled exaltation. Jesus has been placed in an incomparable position of power with God. Matthew thus belongs to the early phase within the resurrection tradition.

Luke and John represent to Wilckens a later phase. Here Jesus appears as early as Easter Sunday before the disciples and in Jerusalem. The question of identifying the risen one with Jesus is more and more emphasized, and is massively demonstrated in the account of the doubting Thomas (John 20:24–29). But John characteristically preserves a critical distance from what he writes; this is exemplified in the following words: "Blessed are those who, without seeing, (come to) believe" (Wilckens' translation).[9]

In Emmaus the identification takes place at a meal, and the same is true in the added chapter with which the Gospel of John concludes. The characteristic motif of mission is also present in this later piece of tradition. The curse, which had weighed so heavily on Peter, is removed, and he solemnly receives his exceptional task. Wilckens is one of those who holds that the somewhat similar story of the "great draught of fishes" in Luke (5:1–9), where Peter is called to be a "catcher of men," equally belongs to the tradition after Easter.

Whereas the oldest tradition "in all its breadth" has understood the resurrection and exaltation as one and the same thing, this identification of the two disappears in Luke. For him the revelations of Jesus are, first and foremost, evidence of his bodily resurrection. The risen one is for the time being here on earth. The ascension, a theme which might have been in existence before Luke, he records in two "not essentially differing" texts (Luke 24:50–52; Acts 1:2–11). Whereas the gospel places the ascension on Easter Sunday, Acts has it taking place after forty days (a symbolic number). Thus Luke, contrary to an earlier tradition, sharply distinguishes between the resurrection and the ascension. His account of the ascension in Acts was inspired in its form by the Old Testament rendition of Elijah's ascension to heaven (1:10).[10]

In his final chapter,[11] Wilckens deals with the origin and meaning of the proclamation of the resurrection in the New Testament. In respect to the origin, there are primarily two texts to take into consideration: the empty tomb in Mark, and the visions of the risen one. Scholars are in general agreement that Peter experienced a vision in Galilee similar to the one Paul was later to have; that Peter understood that vision as an admonition to gather the disciples into an eschatological congregation; and that he thereby became the "rock" upon which the church was to be built (Matt. 16:18). When we speak of visions in the oldest tradition, they are best understood as legitimations for those who were given the authority to assume leadership in the growing church—the prerequisite of leadership was to have been a witness to the risen Lord. If one asks whether the visions may have caused faith, this can only be so in respect to Peter. If the situation of the disciples was, as Luke says, one of dejection and hopelessness, then the earliest of Peter's visions meant "the breakthrough of a new, renewed faith in Jesus." Wilckens, however, also allows for the possibility that Peter had not or had not totally lost his faith and that his vision was thus a confirmation of the same.

Mark's account of the women at the empty tomb is regarded by many scholars as a late legend. Wilckens puts it in the context of the Passion story, claiming that in its present form it can be described as a cultic legend intended to be read at services. Yet he also claims that it contains a seed of early origin, that the women on that first morning of the week found the tomb vacant and fled for sheer fright. If this be so, there is the possibility that the discovery of the women was not until much later, as a consequence of the resurrection faith of the disciples, given an Easter color. Nowhere is there any mention that the women's discovery resulted in faith in the risen one; the only occasion when anything at all is said about faith in connection with the empty tomb is when John describes the conduct of "the disciple Jesus loved" (20:8). Attempts "naturally" to explain the empty tomb—the disciples stole the body of Jesus, Jesus was only apparently dead, Joseph of Arimathea placed Jesus' body in another grave—lack all trustworthiness. Wilckens' conclusion is: the empty tomb cannot prove Jesus' resurrection, but neither can it be disproved by any other explanation. The historian stands before an event which cannot be clarified.

The "visions" were proof to those who had experienced them. But it lies beyond the historian's capabilities to make a conclusive examination. To ask such questions at all would have been an impossibility for the first Christians. Israelite religion was marked by great openness to the acts and the message of God the Creator; they pointed forward and were verified in the future. The first Christians understood the resurrection in the same way; those few to whom Jesus appeared were called to initiate a mission which corresponded to the new experience they had had in the resurrection.

But such deliberations still do not point to the essence of the resurrection faith of the first Christians. When, in our time, one has wanted to find this essence in the Christians' experience of the presence of Jesus—certainly an essential motif in the development of worship—one still does not reflect what was most deeply at stake for the primitive church. To her, the "revelations" of the risen one were limited to a few, and a reunion was not expected until the final period of "fulfillment." When Bultmann says that Jesus had risen in the word of proclamation about the crucified one, he certainly touches upon a central Christian theme.

Yet neither does this reflect what was essential for the primitive church—without the resurrection the cross had, to use Paul's word, no power. The essential thing for the primitive church lay in the mighty act of God through which he raised and exalted "his representative." Jesus represents God—God's love—and love, in a biblical sense, is an act which benefits others and which is made complete by sacrificing one's life for others. Faith in the resurrection of the crucified one "means that no other power but love will reign."

The result of the investigation up to this point, writes Wilckens, is that we have looked at resurrection faith as a historical enigma. Can anything further be said? Yes: that everything concerns *Jesus of Nazareth*. The visions convinced the disciples that God had recognized and verified Jesus, his proclamation and his ministry. The essential thing is *who* this Jesus was and what he had done. Wilckens then gives a sketchy description of the "historical Jesus," of his proclamation of the presence of the kingdom of God, and of how he dealt with man on behalf of this kingdom of God (Wilckens refers to Braun's work on Jesus). "Jesus' proclamation of the presence of the kingdom of God, is, actually, a sermon on love as the ultimate, definitive power." God having said his *yes* to Jesus, "man's relationship to God is principally and unchangeably determined in his relationship to Jesus."[12]

Wilckens concludes with a few words about the truth of the resurrection. What originally happened or might have happened cannot be verified by an isolated historical statement. No demand can be made that someone, against all reason, must "believe" that the impossible happened through God's omnipotence. In neither case is justice rendered to the testimony and experience of the primitive church. For the truth of the testimony manifests itself not by an isolated reference to the past, but by reference to what is happening, to the historical consequences the event has and still continues to have.

Research and the Question of Continuity

We must face the question of the relationship between the earthly Jesus and the primitive church's faith in Christ—a question which also includes the issue of the importance attributed to the received picture of the earthly Jesus. The problem became of immediate interest as soon as the historical-critical method appeared on the scene, and has not since ceased to occupy theology. It is, of course, possible to undertake Jesus research without bringing up this matter; in many of the works we have dealt with, the problem has not been broached. But a great deal can be learned from a few scholars who, directly or indirectly, have dealt with the issues.

The background of the Christology of the primitive church is its resurrection faith, the certainty that the crucified one has risen and that God thereby has recognized Jesus and the fulfillment of his ministry in his death. In light of what we have previously heard of Braun's conception of the resurrection and his view of the christological titles, it may seem that he severs every connection between Jesus and the faith in Christ of the primitive church. But actually there is for Braun also a continuity between them. We recall Braun's question: has Jesus only proclaimed "radical grace," or is his person, and man's relationship to him, an "indispensable part" of that proclamation? Viewing the Jesus who here on earth grants the forgiveness of sins, Braun chooses the latter alternative. Whether radical grace is bound to the person of Jesus and functions through him in his ministry is not a peripheral question to Braun; it is a question of what is at the very heart of the matter. He has clearly indicated this in a few of the last sentences of his book. The word "God" had many meanings in Jesus' time. Man's relationship to God could involve a duty to hate other men; it could also mean that salvation was to be earned through obedience. "Every investigation in this book," writes Braun, "has aimed at clarifying that Jesus does not interpret God as a duty to hate, but to love; Jesus does not interpret God as an authority before whom anything can be earned, but rather as the act through which future and hope are given evil and despondent men."[13] There is a continuity between the earthly Jesus and the Christ of the primitive church inasmuch as Jesus in both instances stands at the center—in one case with immediate and still-functioning authority, in the other with an authority determined by the christological titles. Braun apparently has, without directly saying so, removed himself quite far from the master of form criticism, Bultmann, to whom the earthly Jesus was a piece of prehistory; to Braun Jesus is the center, and a permanent authority.

In Dodd, there is no direct discussion of the relationship between Jesus and the primitive church, but the very unusual title of one of his most popular books betrays his view of the matter; Jesus is "the founder of Christianity." One has a strong impression, while reading Dodd's book, that he is ultra-cautious with every word—and the title is certainly no exception. It is clearly programmatic. The Jesus described is totally other than a mere prehistory. All of Dodd's arguments are placed under the aspect of continuity, a continuity which, with Jesus at the center, stretches both forward and backward. However sharply Jesus judges Israel, this does not prevent "the new covenant" from being a continuation and a completion of the old covenant. The circle of friends which gathered around Jesus is the beginning of the "new people of God," which also—with a name which confirms the retrospective continuity—is called "the new Israel." For the inner group around Jesus, the crucifixion "had emptied life of all meaning." But Easter meant a reawakening and a rebirth of the new people of God. Next to the proclamation "Christ is risen" stands "the hardly less basic" confession of faith "raised with Christ" (Col. 3:1). The appearances of the risen Christ, which were "utterly convincing," took place during a limited time. They ceased, but they were replaced—as the entire New Testament is witness—by another and permanent presence of Christ; and it is this permanent presence of the Lord which is "creative of a new corporate life." In other words, he is himself "the continuity" in what happens.[14]

Davies' reflections about the relationship between the earthly Jesus and the proclamation of the primitive church most immediately concern the Gospel of Matthew. We recall that the question of whether Matthew had departed from "the mind of Jesus" could not be answered with a simple *yes* or *no*, according to Davies. "By gathering together the words of Jesus and isolating them, to some extent, and presenting them as a unified collection constituting a 'law' in an external or independent sense, he has made it possible for many to isolate the ethical demand of Jesus from its total setting as part of the Gospel and has thus distorted awareness of that demand. But certainly Matthew never intended to do this." He placed the Beatitudes at the beginning of the "Sermon on the Mount" so as to put everything under the perspective of the gift and of "grace"—he has to a certain extent avoided a purely legalistic interpretation of Jesus' message. What Davies above all desires to say in his final words is that the strong accent Matthew puts on Jesus' ethical proclamation is an important and indispensable ingredient in the entire message of the New Testament. "Grace" can also be isolated. Certain Pauline sayings can be interpreted or mis-interpreted in this way. The New Testament *kerygma* of the death and resurrection of Christ needs the protection of Jesus' ethical procla-mation in order to avoid becoming an abstract formula. When Davies speaks about this, he is not only thinking of different instances in the New Testament, but also of what has happened in the history of the church and what may still happen—Bultmann stands as a model for Davies.[15]

Starting from the thesis that we possess a certainly limited but real knowledge of the "historical Jesus," Norman Perrin devotes the final chapter[16] of *Rediscovering the Teaching of Jesus* to a detailed discus-sion with German and English scholars, concerning what importance this factual knowledge might possess. He refuses assistance from the so-called new hermeneutic launched by a few German and American theologians. He finds—not without reason—that this position is an unclear compromise of Christian faith and the picture of the historical Jesus—it has a clear tendency to blur the distinction between assertions made by historical scholarship and assertions which can only be made on the basis of faith.

Historical knowledge can be used to test varied representations of Jesus, different faith-images. The representation of the old liberal theology proves in certain fundamental respects to be incompatible with the knowledge we possess today. Analogously, contemporary interpretations—for example, of Jesus as a revolutionary or as an Es-sene—can be tested. The results of scholarship can play both a positive role, by providing a "faith-image" with necessary content, and a criti-cal role, by revealing erroneous interpretations. Finally, Perrin claims that there exists a parallelism between men's attitudes to Jesus during his earthly life and their situation in the primitive church. In both cases, the appeal for a new relationship to God in the light of a decisive act of God—as in the light of Jesus and the kingdom of God, so also in the light of the Christ-*kerygma* of the primitive church. In both in-stances, the believer finds himself in the same basic situation; anyone who receives the church's Christ-*kerygma* stands in the same relation-ship to God as did the Galilean disciple who accepted Jesus' proclama-tion of the kingdom of God.

Notes

1. Herbert Braun, *Jesus* (Stuttgart: Kreuz, 1969), pp. 146–58.

2. C. H. Dodd, *The Founder of Christianity* (New York: Macmillan, and London: Collier-Macmillan, 1970), pp. 166–67.

3. Joachim Jeremias, *New Testament Theology*, trans. John Bowden (New York: Scribner's, and London: SCM, 1971), pp. 302–03.

4. Ibid., p. 306.

5. Marcel Légaut, *Introduction à l'intelligence du passé et de l'avenir du christianisme* (1970), pp. 54–55.

6. Jeremias, *New Testament Theology*, p. 308.

7. Ulrich Wilckens, *Auferstehung: Das biblische Auferstehungszeugnis historisch untersucht und erklärt* (Stuttgart: Kreuz, 1970).

8. Ibid., p. 146.

9. Ibid., pp. 43ff., 72–73.

10. Ibid., pp. 91ff.

11. Ibid., pp. 145–69.

12. Ibid., pp. 166–67.

13. Braun, *Jesus*, p. 170.

14. Dodd, *The Founder of Christianity*, p. 171–72.

15. W. D. Davies, *The Sermon on the Mount* (Cambridge: Cambridge University Press, 1966), pp. 149–50.

16. Norman Perrin, *Rediscovering the Teaching of Jesus* (New York: Harper & Row, and London: SCM, 1967), pp. 207–48.

7

RESULT AND COMMENT

A number of contemporary scholars have now reported their find-
ings. Questions have been raised concerning what might be historically trustworthy. None of the scholars we have dealt with has been
able to write a biography of Jesus or make the earthly Jesus the object
of psychological analysis. Such attempts lie beyond the possibilities of
historical-critical research and are doomed to fall. There is no direct
information about Jesus' life before his "public ministry," and there is
neither a way of determining how long this period lasted nor even a
possibility of ordering its events in a fixed time-sequence. What can
be said is only that the point of departure for his ministry seems to
have been his baptism, administered by John the Baptist, and that his
earthly life ended on the cross, after the death sentence by Pontius
Pilate, in the year 30 or possibly 33 A.D.

This by no means indicates, however, that the earthly Jesus is to be
seen only as a mocking shadow, fading into an impenetrable dusk. In
reality, scholarship testifies to highly essential matters: to his central
message, to his pattern of behavior, and not least, to such things as
have given offense to many. Yet important questions still remain
unanswered.

Our concluding commentary must chiefly address itself to two questions: the ethical perspective, and the kingdom of God. In both cases
we deal not merely with Jesus' proclamation but also with his deeds.

The Ethical Perspective

To speak of "Jesus' ethics" is anachronistic—wrong associations are a
temptation. Expressions such as "the ethical proclamation" or the
"ethos" of Jesus may possibly be acceptable. More precisely, one might
say that the purpose of his proclamation was to reveal how human life
ought to be lived in accordance with the will of God. At this point

there is great unanimity. We may dare claim on good grounds that in all essential matters we possess a historically trustworthy picture of Jesus' ethical teachings. We have already provided two summaries of scholarship: first of all, in comparing the conclusions reached by scholars following differing angles of approach; secondly, in connection with an analysis of the importance of "discipleship" as a pattern for living. In our final treatment we must attempt to make them the object of more intimate analysis.

Jesus' ethical proclamation is least of all a conglomerate of different commands and rules. It has an obvious center, a point which decisively influences everything he says about individual ethical questions. This is the radical love commandment, viewed from a twofold point of view as "love of God" and "love of neighbor." The significant thing for Jesus is that the command of God is both concentrated on and realized in one's relationship to the neighbor. That one's relationship to God subsequently takes many other forms—acceptance of his love, prayer, gratitude, praise—goes without saying. It is quite natural that Jesus' ethical teaching as encountered in the gospels deals chiefly with the "neighbor," or in other words, with corporate life in the world. However, this does not at all mean that one's relationship to God plays a secondary role: "love of God" is the self-evident presupposition and starting point for common life in the world. The important thing is that the love commandment has absolute priority. Commands, rules, and regulations must give way at the very instant they block the mutual service that love demands in the corporate life of persons. In comparison to this "command," all others become secondary, "relative" and "trivial."

It is from this point of view that Jesus' attitude to the Old Testament and contemporary Judaism must be understood. The Old Testament was Jesus' Bible, and his message proves his profound familiarity with its contents. Jewish scholars have recently devoted great attention to Jesus and his relationship to his Jewish heritage. It is well worth listening to what they have to say. In the French collection *Jésus*, Robert Aron has written an article entitled "La terre qui forma Jésus," a summary of his earlier book, *Les années obscures de Jésus*.[1] Aron attempted to reconstruct both the religious education Jesus may have been given in his home and the instruction he might have received in the synagogue. David Flusser, professor at the Hebrew University in

Jerusalem, has written *Jesus*, in which he stresses that the sayings of Jesus clearly indicate that he "was far from uneducated. He was perfectly at home both in holy scripture, and in oral tradition, and knew how to apply this scholarly heritage. Jesus' Jewish education was incomparably superior to that of St. Paul."[2] The comparison with Paul is perhaps debatable, but the words about Jesus are undoubtedly valid.

We have already mentioned the work of Geza Vermes, *Jesus the Jew*. Above all else, Vermes views Jesus as a Galilean *zaddik*—"Jesus the helper and healer, Jesus the teacher and leader, venerated by his intimates and less committed admirers alike as prophet, lord and *son of God*." "Lord," *kyrios*, was a title of reverence used in relation to exorcists and wise teachers. The term "son of God" reflects the pure and intimate contact of piety with the heavenly Father. Vermes's book undertakes what the author describes as the first part of a larger work in which he will investigate "the genuine teaching of the Master from Galilee." A hint of how he conceives of this are these words which Vermes uses to describe "the Master": "Second to none in profundity of insight and grandeur of character, he is in particular an unsurpassed master of the art of laying bare the inmost core of spiritual truth and of bringing every issue back to the essence of religion, the existential relationship of man and man, and man and God."[3]

In the Sermon on the Mount, Matthew has Jesus say: "Think not that I have come to abolish the law and the prophets: I have not come to abolish them, but to fulfill them" (5:17). Such words quite explicitly reflect Jesus' attitude to the Old Testament. The verse which follows immediately—"Not an iota, not a dot, will pass from the law"—must, however, be attributed to Matthew or the tradition of the primitive church, since the words all too evidently stand in opposition to what must be conceived as authentic for Jesus. If it had been Jesus' intention to "fulfill" the once-given law, he clearly did not mean to add new commands to the old ones. He intended, rather, a sweeping reform in which the primacy of love would be brought forth with sovereign certainty.

Flusser, as mentioned, asserts that Jesus was well-versed in the "oral tradition" alive and current at his time, which was primarily represented by "the scribes and the pharisees." What role can this oral tradition have played for Jesus? His relationship to the pharisees was, as we have seen, a twofold one. He found in them tendencies to interpret the

137

law much as he did himself, yet his encounters with them were marked by an incomparable sharpness.

Even though there were tendencies among the pharisees similar to Jesus' proclamation, they were still not sufficiently influenced by this interpretation of the law to let it determine their attitude to life. The main part of the "oral tradition" had a totally different character. It consisted in detailed rules and regulations concerning the proper observance of the Sabbath, cleansings, sacrifice, fasting, tithing, and so forth. All of this was secondary to Jesus. He did not forbid rules, but in the presence of merely formal and casuistic observance he was biting: "You blind guides, straining out a gnat and swallowing a camel." Without the slightest hesitation Jesus brushed all observance aside if it hindered the demands of love.

The content of Jesus' radical demand is made concrete by the meaning he gives to "discipleship." This does not only concern the inner circle of disciples who "left everything" and literally followed him. A definite word comes to the fore here: to serve. Just as Jesus served his fellow men, so must also his followers—with total readiness for any sacrifice that might come as a result. Such a discipleship means a reevaluation of all values.

One of the most significant things in Jesus' ethical teaching is that "loving God" must be realized in "loving one's neighbor." The word "love" is worn and has many meanings. It can easily lead our thoughts astray, and it is therefore most important to understand what is actually meant. "Loving God" means primarily in this context obeying the will of God. "Loving one's neighbor" means neither infatuation or sentimental compassion, but above all a caring and an attentiveness which expresses itself in practical deeds, whose basis is men's open hearts toward one another and toward the demands for a life together. The decisive thing was that God's ethical demands were to be fulfilled within the human community. Here Jesus could refer to the words of Israel's prophets: to Micah when he said that the pharisees neglected "the weightier matters of the law, justice and mercy and faith" (Matt. 23:23); and to Hosea: "I desire mercy and not sacrifice" (Matt. 9:13; 12:7). God is, to quote Gerhardsson, "not very interested in sacrifices made only to himself, but more so in mercy—i.e. care for one's fellow men."[4] But even though Jesus made references to what had earlier been the general rule in Israel, it nevertheless was a revolution when

138

he radically and consistently claimed that obedience to God's will must be realized in care for one's fellow man—with all the stress upon the human level.

A revolution of this kind testifies to a totally sovereign attitude to an interpretation of the law once given—the same sovereign attitude also meets us in Jesus' proclamation of the nearness and presence of the kingdom of God.

The question that now calls for an answer concerns how extensive this ethical perspective was to be. Matthew presented Jesus' "Sermon on the Mount" as messianic law, as the Messiah Jesus fulfilled the Law of Moses. According to the evangelist, Jesus spoke here to his disciples as well as to the crowd (Matt. 5:1, 7:28). This gospel was addressed to the young Jewish-Christian church which existed in Palestine and its vicinity during the latter part of the first century. Our inventory of Jesus research has shown how Jesus' radical proclamation was adapted and at points modified by Matthew to the situation of this church. But even though Matthew conceived of Jesus' "Sermon on the Mount" as messianic law given to the growing church, it could hardly have been his intention that the law which Jesus preached should be limited only to the "church." It was also intended for people in general as well as for the religious leaders who opposed him. And furthermore, if this radical proclamation of Jesus was a reflection of "God's will," it thereby must have had universal validity. In the vision of "the last judgment" (Matt. 25:31–46), where "all nations" are tried, it is the attitude to life, self-forgetting solidarity with different kinds of human needs realized in practical deeds, which determines the outcome of the decree. The fulfillment of the demands of Jesus is, in other words, a determining factor at the last judgment.

When this view of the last judgment is applied to "all nations," it seems to presuppose that deeds of the kind which the text describes refer not only to those who have been clearly informed as to God's demands, but to all men. It is in this spirit that Gerhardsson comments on the text: "When Jesus reasons as he does in the parable of the last judgment he presupposes that God has a general covenant with man and instills mercy and responsible care in his heart, not only within the particular framework of the 'covenant' but also in some more general way. How Jesus conceives of this general connection between the Creator and mankind is, however, not altogether easy to see."

139

Alongside this statement, the following words by the same author ought to be mentioned: "Jesus saw no sharp dividing-line between that which man had received from God at his creation and that which he had received from him through proclamation, instruction, education or other influences within the fellowship of God's people."[5] In the first citation there is a reference to God's hidden interaction with man—he instills mercy and responsible care into the hearts of men; in the latter quotation the stress is upon what man received at his "creation." There need not be any contradiction between these two points of view; rather, they complement each other. That "it is not altogether easy to see" what Jesus thought of these matters cannot be contested—there is no direct testimony regarding this matter. One thing, however, ought to hold good: if one says that Jesus with intuitive certainty describes what the "will of the heavenly Father," is like, the image of the Creator immediately becomes of interest. The Creator and creation are the self-evident background for all of his proclamation: it is the will of the Creator for his creation that Jesus wants to reveal when he preaches what it means to "do the Father's will." It is thereby evident that Jesus' ethical perspective is universal.

Before we leave this subject, an additional observation remains to be made. A crucial issue has been raised by Braun: what is it that even in our present era gives authoritative power to Jesus' ethical message as we encounter it in his radical demand for "neighborly love," and as he demonstrates his own obedience in his offensive care for the weak and ostracized? Braun's answer is that Jesus' authority cannot be derived or motivated by the christological titles of honor bestowed on him—not, for example, by saying he was "God's son" and assuming therefore that every word that he said or that the Bible had put into his mouth must have an absolute and binding character. The real reason for the authoritative power in the message of Jesus lies in the contents of the message and in its power to convince. It was so during Jesus' days here on earth: "he taught them as one who had authority" (Matt. 7:29). This—and only this—is "true authority." The same applies today: his authority lies in its power to convince, a power possessed by the interplay of Jesus' words and deeds. This implies that his message becomes relevant as a result of dialogue between Jesus and those who listen to him, although this does not mean that every individual word of Jesus therefore possesses timeless relevance.

140

One ethical maxim which Braun questions is Jesus' words concerning the indissolubility of marriage. The edge in Jesus' words is directed toward the discrimination against women in his time: they were totally left to the arbitrariness of men, who had the right at any time to give a decree of divorce. Matthew tried to rescue something of the masculine privilege by adding that the man could give a decree of divorce when the woman had committed adultery (19:10). We sense, writes Braun, the distance which exists between Jesus' rigorous marriage ethic and our present feelings and thoughts; many of us are hard to convince.[6]

It is true, of course, that Jesus' unconditional commands must be seen in relation to the situation in his own milieu, and equally it must be seen that the edge is directed against the discrimination against women. In this respect our own situation is radically different. Braun speaks in general terms of our feelings of distance and of our difficulty in being convinced. Could this matter be looked at from more basic points of view? One could perhaps ask the following question: how do we deal with a marriage which functions in such a way that it is totally destructive of the lives of two people in relation to Jesus' "fundamental command" for mutual care and love, and to what consequences can this confrontation lead?

My comments on Jesus' ethical proclamation as it appears in the light of contemporary research can now properly conclude with a word about the relation between his "fundamental command" and other existing imperatives. The fundamental command can briefly be summarized in this way: obedience to God is effectuated through care for one's neighbor. This radical command clearly has priority in relation to everything else. It is decisive in terms of all that we do in serving one another. It is this perspective which gives Jesus' ethical proclamation its dynamic power. This power destroys all formal or ritual observance of the law; it strikes man at a far more profound level. It has a clearly definite goal, but even when the goal is in sight it forces forth new deliberations in new situations and thus creates new duties, new "commands."

The Kingdom of God

If we reflect on what contemporary research says about the kingdom of God, we can, to begin with, state that there is considerable agreement in certain essential areas. The kingdom of God—in Matthew the "kingdom of heaven"—is the word above all other words in Jesus' proclamation. It is the central content of the "gospel" which he preaches. This kingdom of God is "near"; it is about to break forth; it is indeed present in an anticipatory way in the person of Jesus and his ministry. But that which happens in this present world is only a beginning of that which will, in the near future, take place when God lets his kingdom appear "in all its power." In the foreground of all this stands the fact that Jesus not only proclaimed the coming kingdom of God but also bound its "coming" to his own person and ministry. To proclaim the arrival of the kingdom of God is in itself, as Jeremias stresses, without analogy.[7] Israel's prophets could compromise by saying that God wanted to restore Israel; they could also ominously predict that the "day of the Lord" was near and that God would judge his renegade people. The Qumran sect and others in Jesus' time could give vent to their expectation and certainty that a revolutionizing transformation was about to take place. But none of these said what Jesus did: "Behold, the kingdom of God is among you." Even less had anyone dared to behave and act as God's authoritative steward of the proclaimed kingdom. This unique position of Jesus appears clearly in contemporary research—regardless of one's position toward the christological titles of honor. Just as this position manifests itself in Jesus' sovereign interpretation of the radical love command, it also shines forth in his proclamation of the nearness and presence of the kingdom of God, but above all it shines in his ministry, in the deeds which he performs on behalf of the kingdom—that is, on God's behalf.

"The gospel" is not a piece of instructional material that can be separated from the person of Jesus and allowed to function on its own. Braun, who in many respects is extremely radical and skeptical, declares, in conscious opposition to Harnack's turn-of-the-century view, that Jesus "belongs to the gospel he preaches," and he then bears in mind that Jesus granted forgiveness of sins to man: the gospel is realized in the deed. Among scholars there are variations on this theme: in his ministry to the people, Jesus incorporates the gospel; he is "himself" the gospel; in him the proclaimed kingdom of God has begun to function.

The stress is on Jesus' acts. What did Jesus mean by the "kingdom of God?" We have no didactic explanation, but he demonstrates in his conduct what the kingdom means to him, and he illustrates it in his parables. Some of the parables are intended to defend his own conduct. Others (for example, the parable of the soils), reflect the different ways men react when confronted with his message. A third category (including, for example, the parables of the pearl and the treasure in the field), describes how men discover what the kingdom is all about and how they act in consequence of their discovery; a fourth category speaks of the kingdom of God in images from the world of nature. Everywhere it is a question of a happening; the dynamic character of the Hebrew expression for the kingdom of God radiates everywhere, an expression which cannot be rendered satisfactorily in translation; everywhere it is a question of how the reign of God makes itself known in what happens. Nowhere is the kingdom perceived of as a stereotype, an abstract idea. The kingdom of God which is about to break forth is a new deal: God acts in a decisive—an eschatologically decisive—manner. When Jesus in the parables wants to defend *his* conduct, he speaks, as we have said before, of how *God* acts. This does not imply that he is putting himself in God's place, but it undoubtedly means that he views himself as the chosen instrument of God's new deal.

Jesus shows in his relationship to man what this new deal means. His care for man was total. He did not represent a "spirituality" which was indifferent to or disdainful of the body; on the contrary, as an essential part of his ministry he showed a highly realistic care for man's physical ills. His mighty acts of healing were given such importance that they were conceived of as signs which heralded the arrival of the kingdom of God, and they were apparently so viewed by Jesus himself. But such "signs" did not mean that all those who had been healed by Jesus should therefore have become, to quote Matthew, "disciples of the kingdom of Heaven." The texts also speak of those who had been healed and who went away without showing any gratitude (Luke 17:17).

Is it only banal to say that the kingdom of God consists of men? At times there has undeniably been too much one-sided talk about what Jesus, or sometimes God, does, with the result that man has been more or less put in the shade or, rather, regarded as an object simply to be acted upon. This perspective has, of course, its justification, but man is never merely an object; he is at the same time very much the subject of the course of events in the kingdom of God. Jesus comes with an invitation; he appeals to his contemporaries. It is then up to man himself to answer *yes* or *no,* and to accept full responsibility for his decision. Basically it is a question of receiving in trust the gift which is offered. To live in the fellowship of Jesus is to be receptive. The forgiveness of sins is a gift which he gives totally unconditionally and with indescribable generosity. But it lies in the nature of the gift, as the parables so drastically show, that we cannot keep it and passively enjoy it for ourselves: it will be wasted if we "do not forgive your [our] brother from the heart" (Matt. 18:35). To be forgiven means to forgive "seventy times seven": that is, unreservedly and without restrictions. The gift cannot be locked up in the treasure chamber of one's own self; there it will disintegrate. Neither can it be hidden like a talent in the field; there it will rot. One cannot live from it without living it out. To live in the fellowship of Jesus is to be called as his fellow worker in the service of men—and this gives meaning and direction to life.

There are two terms which have often surfaced in our account of the theme of Jesus and the kingdom of God: demonism and apocalypticism. Both motifs are characteristic phenomena stemming from the intertestamental period (roughly 200 B.C. to 100 A.D.). To ask what role these two motifs might have had for Jesus is basically to ask what importance this period with its peculiar issues and atmospheres might have had for him. Jesus research in our time, as we have seen, has conceived of these problems in a variety of ways.

The "demonic perspective" is a firm ingredient of the world of ideas of the intertestamental period. When Jesus happens to speak on this theme, he speaks the language of his contemporaries. Satan is, so to speak, the incarnation of all evil power. The presupposition for the kingdom of God to gain territory is that the power of Satan must be broken—it is this very thing that is taking place when Jesus as "the stronger" conquers the "strong man" (Luke 11:21–22). A militant exegete, James Kallas, desires to make this the point of departure for all interpretation of the gospel of the kingdom of God.[8] In contrast, there are also frequent tendencies to discredit the demonic perspective. Such a critical attitude has especially pointed to the following four points: the motif is primitive; it has come from foreign oriental religions, primarily from Zoroastrianism; it explains, to a certain extent, "the origin of evil"; its dualism attacks the Old Testament image of God.

If we examine these points, our interest is primarily in the last one, which concerns the image of God. When Jesus says that the sick people whom he has healed were possessed by evil spirits this is a diagnosis which, from our contemporary point of view, must seem "primitive," although it must be admitted that this judgment is anachronistic, insofar as our medical insight did not exist in his time. That the idea of Satan as a power opposed to God was formulated in the intertestamental period, under the influence of non-Jewish religions and Zoroastrianism in particular, cannot be contested. But origin and influence cannot in themselves lead to disqualification. The fact is that Jesus used the idea of a demonic power opposing God, and the question of the function of this use remains. Our attempt to explain "the origin of evil" in Jesus and in the Old Testament is of no avail.

Does what Jesus says about Satan and evil spirits violate the Old Testament image of God? That Satan had another position in the New Testament than he had in the Old is unquestionable. In the latter he could be regarded as being in God's service. He is a "prosecutor" and he may well be given the task of testing people such as Job, for example. Even though he may reappear in that role in the New Testament, there he is mainly the enemy, the power bringing destruction and chaos into God's creation. An important and decisive question is whether he thereby violates God's sovereignty.

Jesus speaks without reservations of a power struggle, but there is not the least hint that God's reign was therefore challenged or truncated. When he tells his listeners that he "by the finger of God drives out evil spirits" and that "the kingdom of God is upon you," this in itself is witness to the fact that the reign of God remains intact. In this context it might be of interest to mention that the expression "omnipotent" in respect to God, which occurs frequently in the Old Testament, only occurs in the New Testament (with one exception) in the Book of Revelation. This does not imply any diminution of God's power, but rather that his power is hidden in our era—to become apparent to all when the kingdom of God comes in glory. With this in mind, it becomes confusing to speak here, as has often been done, of a "dualistic" viewpoint; "antagonistic" would be a more adequate term.

Jesus does not polemicize against the Old Testament God, but certain of its long series of sayings about God simply disappear and are unimaginable as coming from Jesus. To a certain extent, the complexity of the demonic element has contributed to this: God is not, as he is sometimes in the Old Testament, one who measures out good and evil, success and destruction, at his own discretion. Ruin and destruction stem not from God's arbitrariness but from a demonic power opposed to God. However, this does not mean that the struggle between good and evil, between God and the enemy, is to be decided, so to speak, over the heads of the people. Among other things, this means that from suffering inflicted upon the individual, the conclusion cannot be drawn that he or she had been "sinners above all others" (Luke 13:1–5). When Pilate put a few Galileans to death and mixed their blood with that of the sacrificial animals, he stands not only in the service of the emperor but also in the service of the demonic power. Even Peter could run errands for "Satan," "possessed" as he was by "the ideal of the Messiah" and its expectations.

However one looks at the terminology of the imagery of Jesus, it can hardly be denied that we are dealing here with hard and fast realities. There are plenty of ideals which lead to disastrous results. This world would not be what it is today if money and status did not function as demonic powers. Hitler's Nazism spread like a demonic pestilence. Racial discrimination is a demonic power with enormously damaging results.

Jesus' relationship to "apocalypticism" has been treated in sufficient detail in two previous passages, one dealing with the presence and future of the kingdom of God, and the other with the meaning of the title "Son of man." The positions of different scholars have shown that we are here on uncertain ground. The expression "apocalypticism" is sometimes stated, without a more definitive examination, to be identical in meaning to "eschatology." It is high time that we now attempt, at least approximately, to indicate what apocalypticism means. Let us begin with the distinction between eschatology and apocalypticism: apocalypticism is a special and particular formulation of eschatology; eschatology has a more general meaning.

Jesus' proclamation of the kingdom of God has a distinctly eschatological slant. He is certain that God will recognize him and give sanction to the ministry he has been called upon to perform on behalf of the kingdom of God. The kingdom of God which had such humble beginnings will ultimately be realized in power and glory. But this does not happen within this era. The kingdom of God is not seen solely as an intrahuman, intrahistorical, "imminent development." Its fulfillment is not of this world. It lies beyond the limits of time and will come into being by God's direct intervention. At the same time it is of importance that that which is to come is seen as a fulfillment of that which has already begun. This also has eschatological content. Jesus is an eschatological figure. It is of decisive importance for eschatological fulfillment how men react to Jesus, to his demands, and to the gift he gives. This eschatological perspective reflects Jesus' expectation; it is part and parcel of the picture and cannot be eliminated without immediately distorting the picture. Is this also true of the apocalyptic?

There was an abundance of apocalyptic literature (*apokalypsis* = revelation) during the intertestamental period. The writings were most often anoymous, although a certain prestige was given to them when they appeared under such names as Daniel, Enoch, or Ezra. They possess an awareness of living in the "end-time," and they depict the revolution which is at hand in gaudy colors and wild imagery. The Revelation of John with its visions, its mythical animal pictures, and its obscure references to contemporary events may serve as an example. Klaus Koch, an eager representative of the importance of apocalypticism, has attempted to describe a few characteristic traits of the movement. World history passes in definite time periods. The last period has arrived and cosmic catastrophe is near. Angels and demons, frequently mentioned by name, often appear as its messengers. The catastrophe leads up to the last verdict—with salvation and painful judgment on opposite sides—for Israel as well as for other nations. The perspective is universal. On the other side of the catastrophe lies paradise, which is conceived of as a return to the innocent time of creation. God's reign is now total. For the restoration to take place there is need for a mediator; this may be a Messiah, a Son of man, a chosen earthly man, or an angel.[9]

A constructive attempt to determine the "essence" of this varied apocalyptic has recently been undertaken by Walter Schmithals. The author deals primarily with the rich literature which flourished within Judaism during the intertestamental period. Terminologically, this apocalyptic had strong points of contact with Persian religion, yet it remained, according to Schmithals, basically "a specific, unitary under-standing of existence."[10] Its view of human history was—in contrast to the Persian view—thoroughly pessimistic and negative; here Satan and demonic powers rule until in the imminent future the kingdom of God breaks in and brings history to its conclusive goal. The book is rich in its observations, but in light of its adoption of an obvious and well-known "existential" pattern, it is difficult not to wonder whether the "unity" in its view of Jewish apocalyptic has not to a certain extent been purchased at the cost of variety.

According to Koch, the importance of apocalypticism, so strongly noted by Schweitzer, was neglected for a few decades, only to be dis-covered in recent years. Koch can certainly refer to a lively discussion of apocalypticism which flared up in Germany around 1960, most im-mediately caused by the apocalyptically-oriented writing of Ernst Käsemann.[11] It is also true that at the present time a reflection of apocalyptic patterns can be found in many areas of life, not least within the world of the arts. But as far as the importance of apocalyp-ticism for Jesus is concerned, the development of scholarship, as we have already stated, has proceeded in the opposite direction. Schweit-zer's view of Jesus as an apocalyptic figure persisted for a long period of time among scholars, but this trend has been broken. It has become more and more evident that the apocalyptic texts in the gospels—the so-called apocalypses of Mark 13, Matthew 24, and Luke 21, as well as parallel passages—stem to a far greater degree from the primitive tradition than from Jesus himself. This does not exclude the possibility that Jesus himself may also have used the apocalyptic imagery com-mon to the time; but even if this were the case, the tradition has embel-lished the language. One example: Jesus undoubtedly, as in the Old Testament, made mention of final judgment; but when Matthew describes the fate of the condemned one with the phrase which appears six times, "there shall be weeping and gnashing of teeth," it is evident that the tradition has added its own colors to the words.

However Jesus used apocalyptic imagery, he undoubtedly expected the kingdom of God to come in its power within the immediate future. Even if not all of these expressions are authentic, and even if Jesus said that "only the Father" knows about "the day and the hour" (Matt. 24:36), he obviously did not reckon that a long span of time would pass before the arrival of the day of fulfillment. Here we must unevasively admit that this expectation was not fulfilled—in any case, not in the way that Jesus expected it. This fact naturally presented great difficulties for the young church, and the New Testament authors reacted in different ways. In Paul's oldest letter (to the Thessalonians) the problem is urgent; Paul explains to his anxious parishioners that those who die before the day of fulfillment will not necessarily suffer a great loss. In the latest Pauline letter (authenticity in certain cases is uncertain) these problems are toned down; he stresses that Christ in his position at the right side of God is "above every name that is named, not only in this age but also in that which is to come" (Eph. 1:21). In 2 Peter the delay is explained with the assertion that for the Lord one day is as a thousand years (3:8). In the Fourth Gospel the problem of the delay is of no significance. The following words are proof of this: "He who hears my word and believes him who sent me, has eternal life; he does not come into judgment, but has passed from death to life" (5:24).

In spite of the fascinating, albeit problematic, role of apocalypticism in the New Testament interpretation, it ought surely to be added that to both exegesis and theology the eschatological hope for the final breakthrough of the kingdom of God, such as we meet it in Jesus, holds good—without being changed by any vague time schedules connected with apocalypticism.

If our report on contemporary Jesus research has shown anything with full clarity, it is that Jesus functioned as the *representative of the kingdom of God which he proclaimed.* He acts on behalf of this kingdom—that is, on God's behalf. In serving this kingdom he assists man physically as well as spiritually; he drives out evil spirits "by the finger of God," and he offers to mankind the forgiveness of sins. He gathers about him the beginning of "the new people of God," "the true Israel." He confirms the fellowship between him and those who receive his message in meals filled with joy and hope, in anticipation of what is to come.

Yet there are, as we have already seen, highly differing opinions concerning the titles of high honor attributed to Jesus in the gospels: "Messiah" and "Son of man." Since I need not again give detailed explanations of these opinions, it will be appropriate to conclude this section with a few general reflections concerning Jesus' view of messiahship.

During all of his ministry, Jesus was constantly confronted with the nationalistic ideal of the Messiah. However, since this ideal was foreign to him, the consequence must have been that the title "Messiah" was, as Dodd says, "an embarrassment" to him. As far as I have been able to discover, there was no other, clearly defined alternative view of the Messiah. Did Jesus himself formulate another such ideal? The picture of the "suffering Servant of the Lord" played an important role for him when he meditated on his destiny, but this does not automatically mean that a new image of the Messiah was in the making. On the other hand, it is obvious that the young church, which looked anxiously for the fulfillment of the Old Testament prophecies, interpreted Jesus as the Messiah on the basis of the suffering Servant in Isaiah. When Dodd claims that Jesus at any rate did not directly refuse "to disown the title," he motivates this by saying "there was no other term available which came near to covering it."[12]

In light of even this problematic relation between Jesus' view of messiahship and his relation to the figure of the suffering Servant, it remains proper to review his own consciousness of his suffering and death. There can be no doubt that when he decided to bring his message to Jerusalem at the time of the Passover, he must have known that this could be fraught with momentous consequences; his disciples were undoubtedly aware of this. Yet the Synoptic Gospels contain comparatively little about the implications of his suffering and death. The essential matters are the repeated predictions about what is to happen, the accounts of the last supper, and the words that the Son of man has come "to serve and give his life as ransom for many" (Mark 10:45; Matt. 20:28). When attempting to find anything of Jesus himself in these texts, scholars are in agreement that they became stylized in the tradition of the primitive church. For example, the ritually stylized formula of the words of institution at the last supper must have appeared at a very early stage.[13] When we meet the formula in 1 Corinthians it is already tradition, and must therefore date from no later than the second decade after the crucifixion.

The very make-up of the texts also causes great difficulties. We know quite well how the primitive church interpreted Jesus' death, but it is far more complicated to find out how Jesus himself looked at the matter. But there is a compass which indicates the direction: Jesus' radical love command, his proclamation of the kingdom of God, and,

not least, his mighty acts on behalf of this kingdom. One of his demands was that one should be prepared, if necessary, to make the
ultimate sacrifice, the sacrifice of life. For himself, this meant to be
"obedient unto death, even death on a cross" (Phil. 2:8). But let us
continue: duty to God, according to Jesus, can only be realized in relation to one's neighbor. Whatever he may have thought in detail when
he sacrificed himself, the words of the texts "given for you" and "as
ransom for many" record a factually correct expression of his view of
his sacrificial act; the uniqueness of Jesus' sacrificial act was that his
sacrifice for others was also a sacrifice *on behalf of the kingdom of God,*
and therefore a sacrifice of universal consequence. To follow the road
of sacrifice to death was finally his only choice. He authenticated his
message and all his ministry on behalf of the kingdom of God with
his sacrificial death.

If one lets the proclamation of Jesus' earthly ministry shed light on
how he may have understood his passion, one can also in that same
light detect what he may *not* have meant. It can hardly have been
his intention to reconcile God by his sacrifice. Such a notion must
seem foreign to one who sees the present breakthrough of the kingdom
of God as God's own act. He did not directly combat the sacrificial
cult in the temple, which surely intended to influence and redirect
God, but he downgraded it, as the prophets of Israel had done earlier.
No New Testament word ever indicates that God was "reconciled"
through Jesus' sacrifice—the classic word is rather: "God was in Christ
reconciling the world to himself" (2 Cor. 5:19). There was never a
question of whether the sacrificial death of Jesus could "redirect" God.
Jesus' concern was to remain faithful unto death to the task which God
had laid upon him; the sacrifice did not concern God, it concerned
man, his "ransom," his liberation from destructive powers, and his
fellowship with God.

This is the focal point: the image of God as encountered in the
proclamation and ministry of Jesus. We recall that Braun and Gerhardsson—let us now say: for good reason—stressed in similar words
the peculiar (Gerhardsson) and the bewildering (Braun) element of
contradiction inherent in the fact that Jesus simultaneously tightened
up God's demands and with radical generosity demonstrated God's
forgiveness. Nothing was more characteristic of Jesus than these two
apparently contradictory attitudes. In his radical demand, Jesus de-

151

clared the will of God the Creator; in his radical forgiveness he demonstrated how God acts—and when this aroused offense, he defended his *conduct* by speaking in parables about how *God* acts. And it was this—how God acts—which was the heart of the matter.

Contemporary moralists criticized Jesus for his demand and his gift. In "the law" it was once and for all stated what one would and could not do. When Jesus forgave sins, it was a blasphemy against God, and his association with "sinners and publicans" was unpermissible laxness in regard to notorious lawbreakers, a glaring disregard for the carefully fixed penance which was the only condition for accepting such people. But Jesus acted in his own way, without the slightest hint that he was conscious of any contradiction between his demand and his generosity.

Jesus did not formulate any "concept of God," nor did he give us any image of God. His conduct speaks for itself, and to use John's words: "He has made him known" (1:18). But he did not do so without being punished. According to the laws he had to expiate his sin by dying. For Matthew, Jesus completely fulfilled—to return to Gerhardsson's interpretation—Israel's old commandment to love God with all one's heart, soul, and might. For Jesus, sacrificial death on a cross was the ultimate proof that he had fulfilled his work and ministry in obedience to God's will; and this was only possible by a sacrifice for others in the service of the kingdom of God.

The Earthly Jesus and Faith in Christ in the Church

The account of what took place immediately after the crucifixion contains drama which cannot be matched. But it also contains extraordinary difficulties for the student of history, and ultimately that which is at the very heart of the matter is inaccessible to scholarship. The texts uniformly assert that the disciples were transformed. At one time during Jesus' days here on earth, he had sent out his disciples to proclaim the kingdom of God; this was now part of a past era—there was nothing more to proclaim. The catastrophe of the crucifixion had in one blow laid desolate everything they had hoped for. But a swift change took place. It was not long before these same disciples reappeared; dejection was replaced by an undaunted and faithful fearlessness. The disciples again possessed "glad tidings" to carry forth.

Something had happened to them; they were assured that Jesus had "risen," that God had awakened him.

The reference to the resurrection was the point of departure for the disciples' renewed proclamation, and, as the New Testament texts confirm, it was the basis for the faith of the primitive church. Thus the factual veracity of the resurrection immediately assumes importance. But this is a question which cannot be answered definitively by historical-critical research alone. That which is directly accessible to scholarship is only that the disciples were firmly convinced that they had met and seen the risen one.

There are, as we know, several problems in the texts: the physical identity of the risen one, the issue of the empty tomb, the "Christophanies" to individuals and/or to masses of people, and so forth. This brings us back to the matter of what is historically accessible, what, in spite of all the questions connected with the accounts, holds good in the Easter stories; and again we can only assert the certainty of the disciples that Jesus had "appeared" to them alive. It is beyond the sphere of historical research to analyze the nature of these experiences, or Christophanies, as they are called, just as it is impossible to disprove what they proclaimed.

The certainty of the disciples, the "witnesses to the resurrection," stems from what must have been their amazing and overwhelming experience. They had been taken by surprise, and their most immediate reaction seems to have been one of fear and joy. To a scholar like Wilckens, who describes the disciples in this fashion only after a detailed and critical examination of the texts, the necessary conclusion is that they were not involved in fabrication, nor were they merely projecting their inner lives. Something had indeed happened.

Even though the texts in question make the resurrection "recognition" dependent on the disciples' reminiscences of events which took place during Jesus' life, and even though they cast Jesus' suffering and death in a totally new light, it must still be acknowledged that the primitive Christian *kerygma* about the crucified and risen one appears in the New Testament as a "unity in diversity." The complex of events—suffering, death, resurrection, exaltation—is presented as a theme with variations.

Against the background of this complex of events appears faith's confession of Christ in the early church as manifested in christological titles of high honor. Among these, "Messiah" was of greatest importance for the primitive church. For the earthly Jesus it had become a risky title because of the prevalent nationalistic idea of the Messiah—and, as Dodd says, "an embarrassment." But this risk no longer existed; it disappeared as messiahship became definitely confined to the sacrificial act on the cross; we "preach Christ crucified" (1 Cor. 1:23). Within the rapidly growing church of the Gentiles, however, "Messiah" did not have the same central importance (in contrast to the Jewish-Christian fellowship), and the equivalent term *Christos* became, as time went by, a proper name: Jesus Christ. In this church other titles of high honor took on importance: above all, "Lord" (*Kyrios* is the translation in the Septuagint of the corresponding Hebrew word for God) and "Son," refers to Psalm 2:7 and 12, where the king is given a sonship of higher order than the children of Israel in general. The word "Son," when used about Jesus, means an exclusive sonship. In both cases it is a question of titles which belong to the divine sphere.

The New Testament expanded this high Christology even further by declaring the pre-existence of Christ and his participation in God's creation. According to Paul, the pre-existent Christ "emptied himself" when he took "the form of a servant" (Phil. 2). In the Gospel of John he is described as the Word (*Logos*)—a formulation which is usually used in reference to Jewish wisdom literature, in which "wisdom" can appear in the form of a person. The Word which was with God and which was God and which functioned at the creation (see also Col. 1:16), "became flesh," incarnate in Jesus Christ.

To the christological building complex belong finally the two accounts of the birth in Matthew and Luke. These accounts have a uniqueness all their own in their mass of poetic symbolism: for example, the visions of angels, the revelation of prophetic dreams, heavenly choirs greeting the newborn child, and a mysterious star guiding the wise men from the east. The very center of these accounts is that Jesus as the Son of God is attached by the operation of God's Spirit to a virgin birth. The weight is upon the divine act of creation through which Jesus, already in the womb, was the chosen one, the Son (it is worth pointing out that these texts stand in total isolation in the New Testament—they do not resonate in other texts, not even in the gospels in which they occur).

154

The purpose of this sketchy review of faith in Christ in the primitive church has been to give some background for a few essential questions which must now be asked. The first concerns the relationship between the Jesus of research and the faith of the primitive church: is there any continuity between the two?

Attempts have been made to come to terms with this problem by saying that the continuity between "the Jesus of history and the Christ of faith" lies in the personal identity which exists between them. Peter gives a clear statement of this in his Pentecost sermon: "God has made him both Lord and Christ, this Jesus whom you crucified" (Acts 2:36). This continuity of identity was self-evident to the primitive church. All the gospels give the same answer when they present Jesus as the Messiah, the Lord, the Son, and so forth. Such an answer may be justified—as far as it goes. But the question of the relationship between *the Jesus of research* and the primitive church has still not been answered—the question has not even been asked. The primitive church did not know of any "Jesus of research." Such a question could only be asked after the historical-critical investigation of the gospels came into being, and this happened—at the outset most gropingly—about two hundred years ago.

This research has met with deep mistrust in the church, and this is understandable. It is due not only to the fact that pictures of Jesus, as Schweitzer pointed out, have changed according to fashionable trends in research. It is also and above all due to the fact that research for a long time, openly and secretly, was marked by a polemical attitude toward the primitive church's faith in Christ: it seemed desirable to present the "teaching of Jesus," as currently interpreted, as a more accessible alternative for modern man. Such tendencies were still common at the beginning of this century. In conscious reaction to all those modernized pictures of Jesus, Schweitzer presented an apocalyptic Jesus, a picture which had the merit of being free from all modernizing tendencies. Ever since, such tendencies have been resisted by historical-critical research. But if Schweitzer held that the apocalyptic elements in the gospels automatically gave a trustworthy picture of Jesus, the situation seemed totally different to the school which subsequently assumed leadership in Germany, exercising international influence—the school of Rudolf Bultmann. The intensive scholarship of this school was marked by great skepticism of the gospel texts. Bultmann and his followers realized at an early stage that one could only have frail knowledge of the "historical Jesus" and his message. What was available was prehistory, and this prehistory proved nothing more than that there was, so to speak, "something historical" behind the *kerygma* upon which the entire weight was put. In this view the continuity between the earthly Jesus and Christian faith is reduced to a minimum.

How does contemporary research deal with this question? The answer must be that the question of continuity is cast in a new light. Previously one had contrasted the proclamation of Jesus with the apostolic proclamation of Christ. From this point of departure, it was difficult to find any immediate and clear continuity between the two. Present-day research also certainly speaks of a proclamation of Jesus; it concentrates on two focal points: the radical command and the radical gospel of the kingdom of God. But this is not everything; the determining factor is that Jesus, in both cases, realizes what he preaches. When, according to Luke, the crucified one says: "Father, forgive them; for they know not what they do" (23:34), his words—whether they are authentic or not—reflect the very radicalism of the demand he proclaimed and realized in his own life. And furthermore, nothing in contemporary research is more evident than that Jesus appeared and acted as "the enigmatic representative of the kingdom of God." He liberates and restores man, mediates forgiveness of sins on behalf of God, and gathers about him a group of people who are to become part of the kingdom of God. He not only proclaims this "gospel"—he embodies it in his own person, making it incarnate. Thus the connection between Jesus in his earthly existence and the early church's faith in Christ is obvious. It is a connection which does not appear with clarity or inevitability as long as one only has Jesus' proclamation in sight, since the proclamation of the primitive church was obviously not automatically identical with that of Jesus. One must look at both the proclamation and the person of Jesus.

The connection between Jesus' life on earth and the primitive church is very complex. The following theses might contribute to some clarity: the situation in the primitive church was different than during Jesus' days on earth, but *the gospel is the same.* Resurrection faith is the most immediate and obvious presupposition for the creation of the primitive church as well as for its proclamation; it meant that God had acknowledged Jesus and his ministry (which culminated in his death) by "raising" and "exalting" him.

After the resurrection the situation changed, but the gospel remained the same. The gospel which the earthly Jesus preached and "embodied" is to be found with a wider perspective in the message of the primitive church. God (God's love) in Christ (Jesus' completed ministry) reconciled the world to himself; with this, God's forgiveness is made available for all times and nations. Furthermore, when the earthly Jesus incorporated those whom he had restored and liberated into fellowship with him under the sign of the kingdom of God, this had its full correspondence in the primitive church. For "faith" in the church is also a life in fellowship with Jesus or Christ (the term is not essential) under the sign of the kingdom of God.

The essence of the young church's faith in Christ was that Christ had come from God and had returned to him, and that it was God himself who in Christ had reconciled the world to himself. Or let us, for a change, listen to a summary of the gospel of the primitive church in Johannine language: "In this the love of God was made manifest among us, that God sent his only Son into the world, so that we might live through him. In this is love, not that we have loved God but that he loved us and sent his Son to be the expiation for our sins" (1 John 4:9-10). Such statements cannot be the object of historical research. Such research has no possibility of saying what God has done. But statements of faith, however, can be made the object of an analysis which intends to clarify their meaning, and this is one of the most important tasks of theology. But that is beyond the purpose of this book.

The Importance of Jesus Research

Of what importance is historical-critical research concerning Jesus? As far as possible, this form of scholarship has tended to give us a picture of Jesus the man. No historical research, least of all research of a person, can pretend to give definite and exhaustive results. Scholarship always stands open to revision—new material appears, and interpretations must be corrected. Such is also the case with Jesus research. In this area, as we have clearly observed, there are issues which are exceedingly difficult to master. This is due to the very make-up of the texts. To write a biography of Jesus cannot be done. Many questions lie within that realm of uncertainty where there is room only for hypo-

thetical answers; other questions cannot be answered at all. Nonetheless I dare say that the historical research that has been reviewed in
this book has given a remarkably unified and historically trustworthy
picture of very essential traits in Jesus' public appearance, proclamation and ministry. Of what importance is this?

The church, as we know, has frequently exhibited a deep mistrust of
historical Jesus research. That a so-called fundamentalist view of the
Bible must reject such research is obvious and needs no comment.
More subtly, however, we have seen that scholars themselves sometimes claim that it is of no consequence, for Christian faith at any rate,
whether Jesus research leads to any result or not; Christian faith sets
out from the *kerygma* of Christ, and it does not matter whether one
knows anything of the Jesus of history or not. The first phrase is correct—but is the second one? Theories of this kind appear, as is demonstrated by the recent book *Jesus Christus in der Verkündigung der
Kirche* by Walter Schmithals, a member of the loosely identified "Bultmann school." The book is not lacking in interest and sharpwittedness,
but it is at the same time an example—by no means unique—of how a
theory can be carried to the point of absurdity. A few examples will
prove the point: "To ask for the historical Jesus may, historically, be
possible and permissible, but theologically it is forbidden [*verboten*].
The church has never been interested in the nature of Jesus' life [*für
das Was und Wie des Lebens Jesu*]." The thought behind this astonishing statement is that after the church was built on the basis of the
kerygma of Christ, there were stories about Jesus' lifetime still in circu-
lation; Mark compensated, however, by placing them within the framework of the *kerygma*. The christological confession had its origin in
the Easter event, which meant "a transition from the expectation of
salvation to the mediation of salvation. The community of the crucified Christ, born after Easter, considered itself an eschatological congregation of salvation. This Peter and Paul, Augustine and Luther,
Barth and Bultmann and all legitimate theology have always thought."
But as soon as "historical thought" made inroads into theology, the
existence of this eschatological community became precarious. That
which at the present time is called "the new quest of the historical
Jesus" has placed the church as well as theology in a very difficult
situation. "For this is the reason, if not the cause, the leading factor
for the de-Christianization and detheologizing of the church today; the

reason for the triumph of the law over the gospel, self-righteousness over righteousness, the human deed over divine grace."[14]

Such statements express an unequivocal anathema against all exegetical research concerning Jesus. According to Schmithals, all the damage that accompanies historical-critical scholarship makes it understandable that such research be declared "theologically forbidden" (however that judgment may be executed); the secular historian alone is allowed to pursue such research, not the theologian. Thereby Schmithals has pushed his theory to absurdity. He has isolated himself, locked up his theology, and cut it off inwardly as well as outwardly.

The task that Jesus research has undertaken is obviously a task of universal significance. The requirements of factual knowledge are the same for the secular historian as for the theological scholar. At stake can be nothing other than to record, without other ends in mind, what can be said about Jesus that is trustworthy. For example, were we to start with the intention of opposing the primitive church's faith in Christ, the work would be compromised from the beginning—as it would also be were we to start with a purely apologetic intent.

It is of great importance that this research be pursued, using every available resource, and that it be pursued from a generally human as well as theological point of view. The place Jesus occupies in the life of mankind demands this. There is neither rhyme nor reason—least of all theologically—for leaving the earthly Jesus to all sorts of free, loose, arbitrary, and quasi-historical constructions. To the extent that a historically trustworthy picture is attainable, it has its rightful place, let me say, in the common corpus of human knowledge.

Historical Jesus research is necessary; its legitimacy is obvious. When one subsequently estimates its importance more closely, it is appropriate to confront the picture of Jesus given by contemporary research with Schmithals's explosive reprimand of scholarship. It is extremely difficult, not to say impossible, to authenticate these violent accusations of Schmithals by the picture of Jesus given in contemporary research. The trend, as we have seen, is directly in the opposite direction. That historical Jesus research has caused problems for the church's proclamation is undeniable, and it may be well to add that the relationship between scholarship and the church can hardly be unproblematic. That is one thing. But it is totally different, in a work published in 1970, to make such accusations. For, paradoxically, such accusations are in basic agreement with the accusations which Jesus, as portrayed in contemporary research, directed against the pharisees and the Judaism of his time. None were more exposed to criticism than those who "trusted in themselves" and in their accomplishments. And nothing is more characteristic of the Jesus uncovered in research than that he himself was the bearer of the gospel he preached, and that he acted on behalf of God's "grace" with a generosity which seemed totally offensive. It cannot be contested that a great many things exist in the church today that support Schmithals's description—in his battle, however, he could find help in historical Jesus research.

There is no denying that a new era began with the apostolic message of the crucified and risen Christ. Neither is there any denying that the young church which grew forth understood itself as an "eschatological community of salvation," to use Schmithals's terminology. The entire New Testament bears witness to this community's faith in Christ. The center of this testimony is that everything said about Jesus concerns God's purpose for him, God's activity in and through him: that which has already happened, that which is still happening, and that which will happen. *God* in Christ has "dwelt among us," and thereby it has been revealed "who *God* is": *God* in Christ has reconciled the world unto himself and has opened loving arms to the world; *God* has exalted Christ and given him the name above all other names— therefore neither death nor life nor anything else "will be able to separate us from the love of *God* in Christ Jesus."

Schmithals's attack on historical research gives us cause to add a few remarks to what has already been said about the relationship between faith in Christ and historical Jesus research. First, without this faith in Christ we would scarcely have had any knowledge at all of Jesus, and indeed, if we had heard anything about him, it would have been merely a random remark about a life which miscarried. Second, if the essential thing for faith is *God's* acts, it goes without saying that the question of facticity (*quaestio facti*) cannot be answered by historical research; the task of research is to concentrate on the *interpretation* of the content and meaning of the given witness of faith. Third, historical Jesus research, whose purpose is to determine what is historically trustworthy, exceeds its authority if it seeks to be the gauge for the faith of the church. In such a case it would forget that its picture of Jesus is not and cannot become a total picture, that the church's faith in Christ builds on presuppositions which were not available during Jesus' lifetime, and that these viewpoints must be considered in every encounter between the Jesus depicted in research and the Christ who is the subject of the church's faith.

The argument that the church should never be interested in Jesus as a person is absolutely untenable. The proclamation of the crucified Christ would lose all its content and meaning and become an abstract construction if it did not matter who this man was, what he wanted, and what he had done. And furthermore, any claim to a lack of such interest is refuted by the existence of the gospels as well as by the fact that the church in its worship has preached upon these texts. The thesis that "theologically" it should be forbidden to ask for "the historical Jesus" is equally unreasonable; this presupposes that at root Jesus was not a real human being at all. But just this—his true humanity—has always been part and parcel of the church's confession. Since, as is well known, theology has had great difficulties in coming to terms with this humanity and has often and in oblique ways suppressed the elements of true humanity which appear in the gospels, it therefore becomes the inevitable task of research as far as possible to give a historically trustworthy picture of Jesus the man.

All historical-critical research counts with relative results. Interpretations can be debated and new material can be uncovered. As far as Jesus research is concerned, our overview has borne witness to limited possibilities and unanswerable questions. But it has also confirmed that research cannot be dispensed with by frivolous comments that one scholar is trying to destroy another. Such is not the case. Results may differ in detail, but with regard to most essential matters there exists an agreement so great that historical trustworthiness is hardly jeopardized. The intensive and methodological work of Jesus scholars merits the same respect as any other careful and serious research. There is every reason to listen to what it has to say.

Let us view the matter in terms of general information. We all have reason to be grateful for the basic knowledge that Jesus research has given us. From the viewpoint of general knowledge, it would be extremely unsatisfactory if the man behind all that has transpired with him at the center were to turn out to be an obscure shadow, a ghost, or a more or less mythological figure defenselessly exposed to bungling manipulations and loosely motivated hypotheses. Such gross possibilities can be tested by the historically trustworthy picture that research has given us of Jesus' proclamation and conduct. And this picture has a rightful home as an obvious part of the common resource of human knowledge. This requires certain things when instruction about Jesus is included, say, in the academic study of religion. Serious utilization of Jesus research guarantees that education deals with essential matters and that questions such as whether or not Jesus walked on water remain secondary.

Yet the most important thing that scholarship has given us with its picture of the earthly Jesus is not an image, to be used as a tool for testing and control. Of incomparable value is what this picture reveals for our own time. In sharper terms, this picture of the Jesus of research lays bare some of the most immediate and overwhelming global problems of our time. And, obversely, this same picture of Jesus speaks sharply to individual persons—to those who are "near" and those who are "far off," to borrow a biblical expression. But such issues I will leave to my readers to face. In our time, the world of the Bible has become closed and strange to many. I claim that scholarship, by having given us a trustworthy and defined picture of Jesus, can contribute to opening closed doors and creating new contacts with the world of the Bible.

During the years that I have worked with contemporary Jesus research, two words have come to stand out: Jesus as the one who *reveals* and the one who *liberates*. Everything that Jesus says and does can be basically described by these two words. His revelation is radical. He exposes all kinds of human illusions, hardness of heart, prestige-oriented success, and, not least, the wrong side of piety—self-assurance and superiority. He thereby also reveals the life that is meaningful—the life that consists of mutual care and service. At the same time he is, in the face of all human need, the great liberator and restorer. When, to the enormous offense of his contemporaries, he stretches out his hand to the most despised of persons and takes them into his fellowship, he answers his angry accusors by telling them stories which show that *God* acts in just that way. And so he reveals who "God" is. At the final crisis he does the same thing when, because of the accusations and for the sake of the kingdom of God, he follows the way of suffering to the final sacrifice.

162

For anyone who seeks him today, he lays down no more conditions or reservations than he did during his lifetime. As in the case of the woman who was healed by a mere touch, the radiance from his life is so strong that anyone who seeks him receives help—to use an image—by touching the hem of his garment.

Notes

1. Robert Aron, "La terre qui forma Jésus" in the collection *Jésus*.
2. David Flusser, *Jesus*, trans. Ronald Walls (New York: Herder and Herder, 1969), p. 18.
3. Geza Vermes, *Jesus the Jew* (London: Collins, 1973), pp. 225, 10, 224.
4. Birger Gerhardsson, *2000 år senare* (Stockholm: Verbum, 1972), p. 77.
5. Ibid., pp. 80, 70.
6. Herbert Braun, *Jesus* (Stuttgart: Kreuz, 1969), p. 77.
7. Joachim Jeremias, *New Testament Theology*, trans. John Bowden (New York: Scribner's, and London: SCM, 1971), p. 33; cf. pp. 96ff.
8. James Kallas, *The Significance of the Synoptic Miracles* (Philadelphia: Westminster, 1961).
9. Klaus Koch, *The Rediscovery of Apocalyptic*, trans. Margaret Kohl (London: SCM, 1972), pp. 28–33.
10. Walter Schmithals, *The Apocalyptic Movement: Introduction and Interpretation*, trans. John E. Steely (Nashville: Abingdon, 1975), p. 210.
11. E.g., Ernst Käsemann, "On the Subject of Primitive Christian Apocalyptic," *New Testament Questions of Today*, trans. W. J. Montague (Philadelphia: Fortress, and London: SCM, 1969), pp. 108–37.
12. C. H. Dodd, *The Founder of Christianity* (New York: Macmillan, and London: Collier-Macmillan, 1970), p. 103.
13. Cf. pp. 79–80 above.
14. Walter Schmithals, *Jesus Christus in der Verkündigung der Kirche* (Neukirchen/Vluyn: Neukirchener, 1972), pp. 73ff.

INDEX OF BIBLICAL REFERENCES

INDEX OF BIBLICAL REFERENCES

99. Jesus' _core_ teaching